Beginning
Fingerstyle
Blues
Guitar

by Arnie Berle and Mark Galbo.

Amsco Publications
New York • London • Sydney

Edited by Roland Ottewell
Interior design and layout by Mirror Mountain Productions

Order No. AM 71390
US International Standard Book Number: 0.8256.2556.4
UK International Standard Book Number: 0.7119.1509.1

Exclusive Distributors:
Music Sales Corporation
257 Park Avenue South, New York, NY 10010 USA
Music Sales Limited
8/9 Frith Street, London W1V 5TZ England
Music Sales Pty. Limited
120 Rothschild Street, Rosebery, Sydney, NSW 2018, Australia

Printed in the United States of America by
Vicks Lithograph and Printing Corporation

CONTENTS

INTRODUCTION

One day back in March of 1988 a young man named Mark Galbo came to me to study jazz guitar. Over the next several weeks I learned a lot about him. He was twenty-seven years old, he held a degree in music, and he was an excellent blues guitarist. He taught at his studio and as a guest clinician at blues festivals. He also performed all over the country at these festivals and in clubs throughout the New York area. He has played with some of the leading blues guitarists of our time, including Etta Baker and John Cephas. This was of great interest to me because although I have been associated primarily with jazz through my hundreds of columns for *Guitar Player* magazine and the many books I have written, I greatly love fingerstyle blues guitar. For a long time I had wanted to write a book on the subject. As time went by and I saw Mark for his weekly lessons, I became more and more impressed with his dedication to the blues, his conscientiousness about everything he did, and his articulateness. I asked him if he would like to collaborate with me on a book. This is the result of that collaboration.

Since the blues falls into the category of folk or "unschooled" music, there has always been a mystique as to how a student might go about learning it. Legends abound about how Robert Johnson learned his craft from the devil or a witch doctor. We know that many bluesmen learned just by hanging around their elders. But most of us don't have that opportunity and have to turn to instructional books.

One type of book contains direct transcriptions of blues solos by the masters. Unfortunately, many are dauntingly difficult and require a rather advanced technique. The advantage to this book is that we will start from the very beginning and gradually work toward greater sophistication. Not only will you learn the technique necessary to approach the works of the blues masters, but you will acquire the tools to make up your own pieces. And if you decide that you want to branch out into other styles of music, the fingerpicking techniques you learn here will give you a good basis for explorations into ragtime, country-and-western, folk, and even classical music.

All you need to start is an ability to play some of the basic open-position chords. If you can't do this, don't worry, as all chord forms used are shown in diagram form. All the musical examples are given in both standard notation and tablature. In order to acquaint you with the true flavor of the blues sound, which cannot be notated, we have included a compact disc. It illustrates most of the material in this book and listening to it as you progress will help to give you a better idea of the sound you should be striving for. Finally, we urge you to listen to as many records as you can find and to attend performances by blues players.

THE ORIGINS OF THE BLUES

Well before the beginning of the twentieth century there existed in America a large body of music performed by black people for black people. It included minstrel shows, work songs, field cries or hollers, and spirituals. However, at some time during the 1890s—no one knows any exact dates—another kind of music could be heard in rural areas of the Deep South. This new music came to be called "the blues" sometime around 1900. Ma Rainey, quoted in Sandra R. Lieb's excellent biography *Ma Rainey, Mother of the Blues*, says that she first heard the word "blues" applied to a song she heard sung by a little girl on a street corner in 1902.

Although the blues emerged from all over the South, many of the most important and influential blues musicians came from Mississippi. There, scores of impoverished, wandering performers accompanied themselves on the guitar at turpentine and lumber camps, roadside cafes, railroad stations, and street corners. Out of many a few were recorded and have become famous among aficionados of early blues. Bluesmen like Charlie Patton, Robert Johnson, Son House, and Bukka White helped develop a style known as *country blues* which has been copied over and over again throughout the world. Country blues were about unrequited love, loneliness, troubles at work, the desire to travel (*I got to keep movin*'), or of specific events. "Backwater Blues" told of a flood on the Mississippi River. Other songs were about legendary personalities like C.C. Rider and Stagger Lee.

The Form

The early street musicians would sing their stories, adapting the musical form to their lyrics. It might have taken them nine, twelve, thirteen, or any number of measures to get through a verse. Their melodies were simple, direct, and elemental; their accompaniments often consisted of nothing more than a single chord or a repeated riff. However, the spread in popularity of the blues led inevitably to its modification and standardization. Ever larger numbers of phonograph owners picked up an interest in the blues and favored records that were to their own tastes. Bands began to play the blues not just as accompaniments but as instrumental pieces. W.C. Handy, who came to be known as "the Father of the Blues," wrote down songs so that they could be published and sold as sheet music. Handy himself receives credit for composing the first blues to be printed. Some people considered that Handy's songs were not real blues, but it is more valuable to think of him as emblematic of the influences that began (and have not yet ceased) to filter into the blues and modify it.

Today, the twelve-measure verse reigns as the classic blues form. And when we speak of a twelve-bar blues we are not just speaking of a number of beats, but also of a definite cycle of chords. As we mentioned above, the early blues singers would often use only a single chord to accompany an entire song. As their melodies became more sophisticated they brought in more chords, borrowing from the simple folk songs and church hymns they knew. The classic pattern uses the chords that are built on the first, fourth, and fifth degrees of a major (or minor) scale. In a major key these chords are the three major chords, and are known as a key's *primary* chords. Forgetting the other chords in the key and using only these three primary chords, it is still possible to harmonize any melody note in the key. Below we see the I, IV, and V chords in the key of A Major.

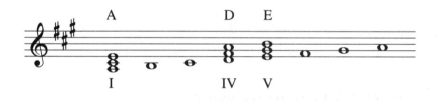

Still, what is special about the blues progression is not the use of these three chords, but rather their arrangement over the twelve measures of the verse.

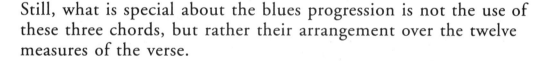

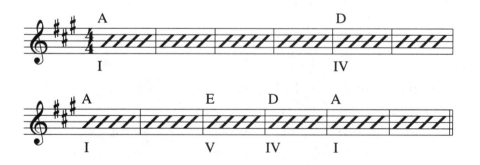

The sound of the above progression is so distinctive and common that anyone who has the slightest familiarity with popular music will recognize it immediately. The example shown above would constitute one complete verse, or chorus, of the blues. The performer repeats it as many times as he wishes.

The Beat

Keeping a solid rhythm is essential to building an authentic solo blues sound. The bluesman intuitively understands that rhythm is of the body and therefore must be expressed by the body during performance. Stomping out the beat with the foot is the most direct and effective technique for accomplishing this aim. In fact, the solo blues player is like a one-man band. The foot will act as drummer, the thumb as bass player, the right-hand fingers as rhythm and lead guitarists, and the player has the voice with which to sing. The early blues performer, usually armed with only an acoustic guitar, was routinely expected to play "dance" music in crowded, noisy atmospheres. He would use his entire body as well as his instrument to capture the crowd's attention and communicate to them his own personal beat. Soon the dancers would be moving to his rhythm and an improvisational give-and-take would occur between musician and dancer, sending the blues song in new directions. The connection between dance and music cannot be overstated to one who would play blues guitar. Try to infuse all the exercises and pieces in this book with a sense of rhythm and expression. Listen to the accompanying cassette to hear how even the most basic exercises can have rhythmic life breathed into them. Only the form of blues music is simple; its passionate content is another matter.

Picking-Hand Technique for Fingerstyle Guitar

The standard classical fingerpicking technique calls for the use of the thumb plus the first three picking-hand fingers. The thumb is used predominantly to pluck the bass notes while the index, middle, and ring fingers pick the treble notes. The pictures below illustrate this picking technique used in this book and on the tape.

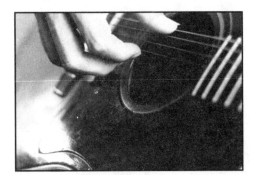
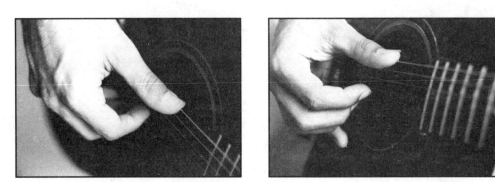

The thumb will usually strike the bottom three strings—E(6th), A(5th), and D(4th)—while the index finger strikes the G(3rd) string, the middle finger the B(2nd) string, and the ring finger the high E(1st) string. The music example below shows how this approach looks in the standard notation and tablature we will be using throughout this book.

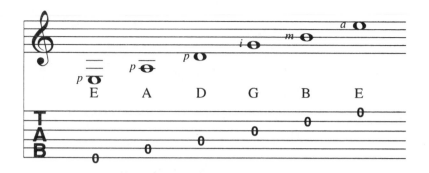

Now we'll move on to some exercises designed to get your picking hand into the correct position. As you play, keep in mind two things: (1) stay relaxed, and (2) strive for a full, warm musical tone. Paying attention to what your ears hear will keep you musical. Notice that both exercises are based entirely on open strings.

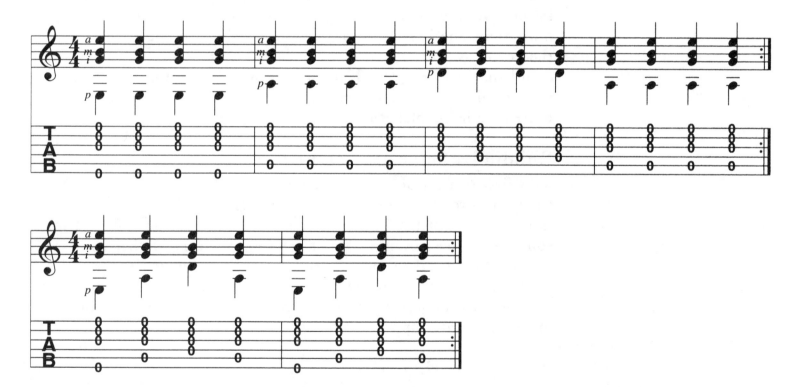

We should note that there are many possible variations on the fingerstyle technique. The Reverend Gary Davis and John Cephas use only their thumb and index finger. Etta Baker picks primarily with her thumb and two fingers. Some players use fingerpicks to obtain a louder, more aggressive sound. Listen to all approaches and follow your intuition. If you already have a style that you are comfortable with, you may certainly apply it to the material in this book. What is important is the quality of the music created.

PREPARING TO PLAY OUR FIRST BLUES

In this section we are going to work up to our first blues. We've chosen the key of A, the same key we employed in dicussing the blues progression. Once again, the three basic chords used for a blues in A are A(I), D(IV), and E(V). The key signature of A contains three sharps—F♯, C♯, and G♯. It is very important to understand that since we will be playing in A and we will be working with chords derived from that key, the key signature for that key will be shown at the beginning of each line of music. It is important to understand this because any chord can be related to more than one key. For example, the D chord is the IV chord in the key of A, but it is also the I chord in the key of D. The E chord that is the V chord in the key of A is also the IV chord in the key of B. You might want to refer to a book on harmony for a more detailed explanation.

Building a Solid Technique

This first section of the book contains studies designed to connect the thumb to the beat of the foot and then to develop independence of the fingers over that steady beat. If you find that some of the beginning exercises are too easy then perhaps you should skip ahead to more difficult material. But if the difficulty of the music ever causes you to lose your steady rhythm you ought to return to the point where you can execute the music without losing the beat. Tap your foot!

The Alternating Bass

The foundation of country blues guitar playing is the rhythmic drive of the alternating bass. Ultimately your playing will only be as good as your rhythmic drive is solid. So let's examine this technique. The first exercise below is based on an open A chord. Although you only play two notes of the chord it's important to finger the complete chord. Notice that the thumb (*p*) is alternating between the root, A, and the note E, the fifth of the chord. Repeat the exercise until you can play it smoothly. Allow each note to ring out clearly. After playing the A be sure that the thumb doesn't touch the fifth string as it comes back to pick the E on the fourth string. While playing with the thumb keep your right-hand fingers in good position: that is, with the index finger (*i*) above the third string, the middle finger (*m*) above the second string, and the annular (ring) finger (*a*) above the first string.

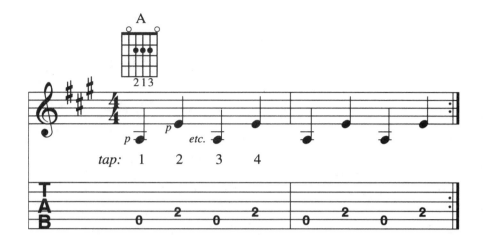

Picking with the Fingers

This exercise is again based on the open-position A chord, with the fingers playing the notes of the chord. You may use the *i-m-a* fingering or any fingering that you feel is more convenient.

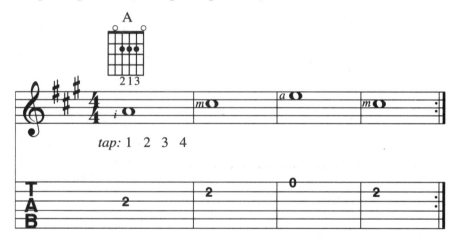

Combining the Thumb and Fingers

In this next exercise try to be precise about synchronizing the thumb and fingers on beat one of each measure. Allow each chord tone to ring for the full four counts.

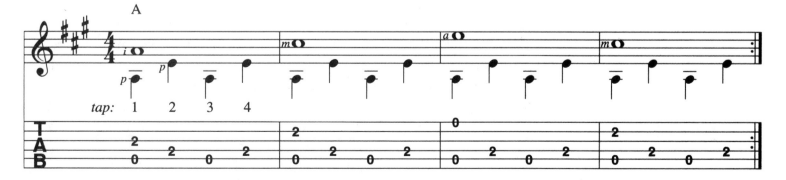

The following exercise is based on half notes played against the quarter-note alternating bass. Again, be sure that the chord notes and the bass notes are synchronized. Tap your foot and keep the rhythm steady.

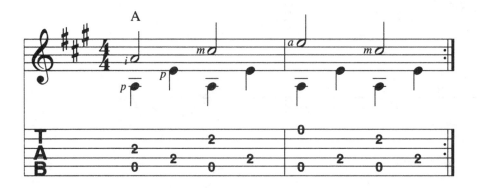

Here you play quarter notes with your fingers against quarter notes in the bass.

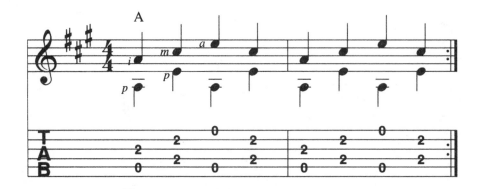

Fingerpicking the D Chord

Below is an alternating bass for the D chord. Notice that the root is played on the second and fourth beats rather than on the first and third. This is because when we listen to the early blues fingerpickers playing this chord we hear that they almost always struck the A (the fifth of the chord) first, followed by the D note.

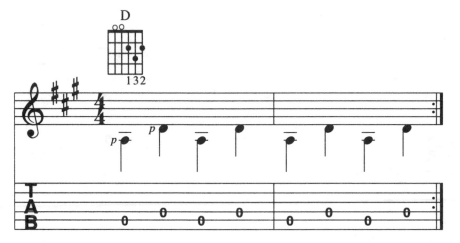

Pick this D arpeggio below as shown. Be sure to hold the chord down well throughout.

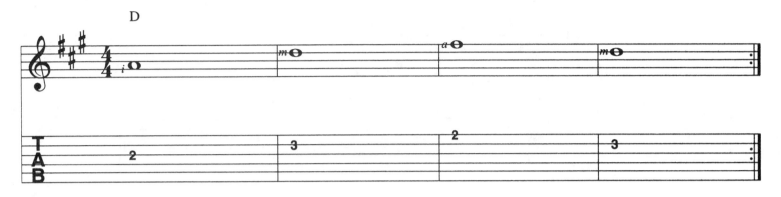

Here we will play the tones of the D chord against an alternating bass.

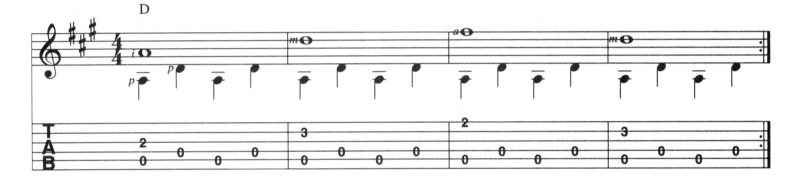

Here we'll play half notes against the bass.

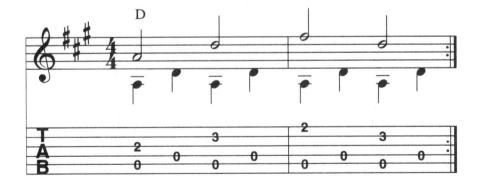

And finally we'll play quarter notes against the alternating bass.

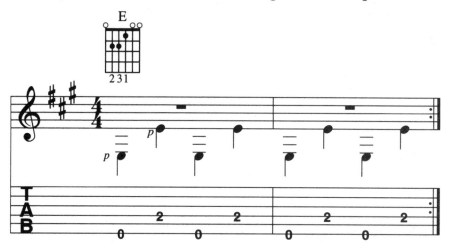

Fingerpicking the E Chord

Below is an alternating bassline for the E chord. Notice that both of its tones are roots. This is not the usual way to play an alternating bass, but the way this chord is going to be used in our first blues song is the same way it is heard on recordings by early blues guitarists. Remember to finger the complete chord.

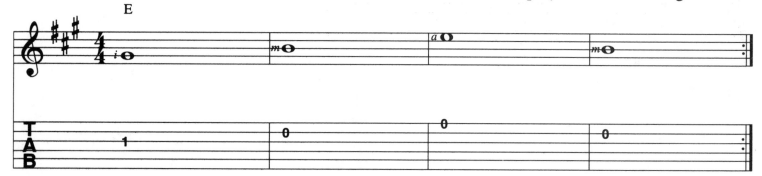

Below are the tones of the E chord as played with the fingers.

The following exercises combine the tones of the chord with the alternating bass. Below are whole notes played against the bass.

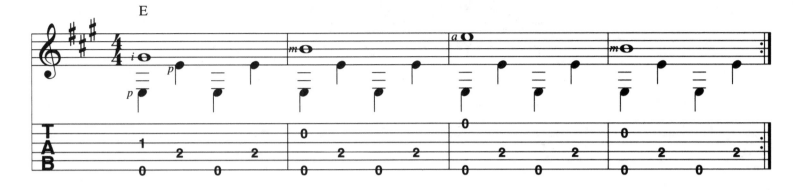

Here are half notes against the alternating bass.

And quarter notes against the alternating bass.

Since we've just practiced the A, D, and E chords, let's now try playing them in the twelve-bar blues form. It's very important that you go smoothly from chord to chord without any hesitation. Play slowly and keep the bass notes steady.

BLUES IN A

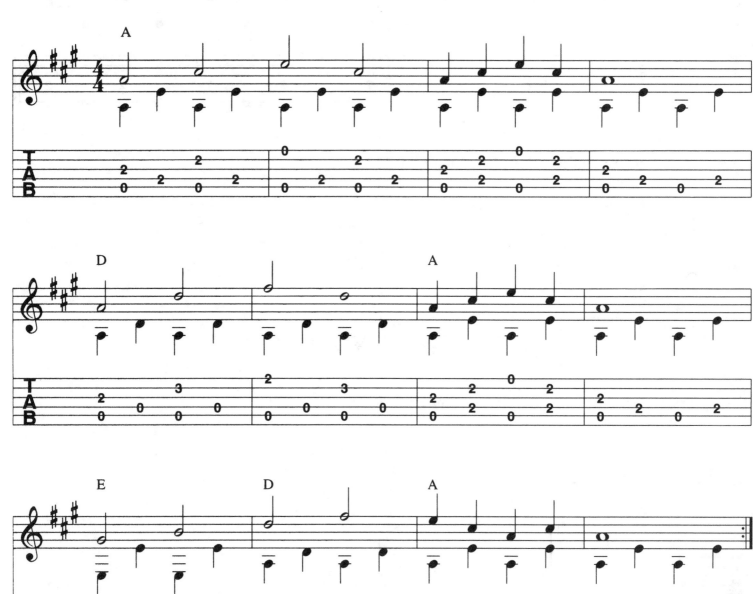

PREPARING TO PLAY A BLUES IN G

The I, IV, and V chords in the key of G are G(I), C(IV), and
D(V). Below are the alternating bass and chord tones for the G
chord. Though this fingering for the G chord is not the most
commonly used, for now it is suitable for our purpose.

Fingerpicking the C Chord

Here are the elements of the alternating bassline and chord tones
for the C chord.

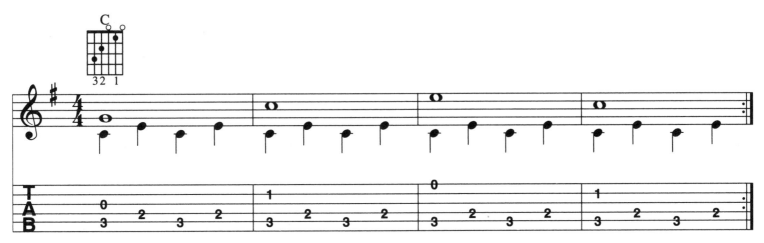

Below is a study based on the twelve-bar blues form using the G, C, chords we've just practiced, plus the D chord we used in the previous section. Play as slowly as you need to in order to keep your beat steady.

BLUES IN G

PREPARING TO PLAY A BLUES IN E

The I, IV, and V chords in the key of E are E(I), A(IV), and
B7(V). Since we already know the fingerings for the E and A
chords, let's work on the B7 chord, employed here as a dominant
seventh chord. A dominant seventh chord contains four distinct
tones—the root, third, and fifth of a major chord, plus a seventh
tone a minor third above the fifth. Although for convenience and
simplicity we have waited until now to introduce it, the dominant
seventh is the most common version of the V chord not only in
the blues but in many other types of music as well.

Here is a study using the twelve-bar blues form with the E, A, and B7 chords.

Twelve-Bar Blues in E

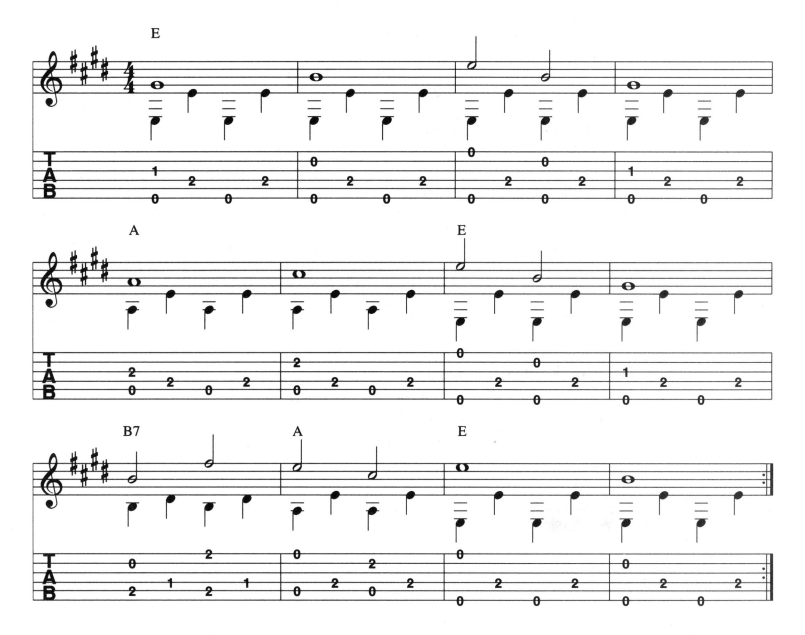

MELODY NOTES

So far the three blues we've played have been made up solely of notes taken from the chords we were holding down with our fretting hand. This of course limits our melodies, so now we are going to increase our melodic potential with the addition of non-chord tones. Earlier we learned that chords come from scales; now we will expand our concept of melody to include all the notes in the scale, whether or not they are in the chord that we happen to be holding down. For some chords we may be able to play all of the notes in the scale while holding down the chord, while with other chords we may be limited to just a few notes of the scale simply because some chord forms make it too difficult to play all of the melody notes. Sometimes if you wish to be able to play more melody notes you may have to finger certain chord forms a little differently than you are used to.

Melody Notes and the A Chord

The following exercise is based on playing the A chord and all its melody notes. It's very important that you hold down the chord throughout the entire exercise while playing the melody notes. Note the new fingering.

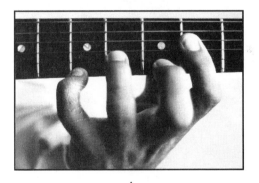

The A Chord, Melody Notes, and the Alternating Bass

In this exercise hold down the A chord while playing melody notes against the alternating bass.

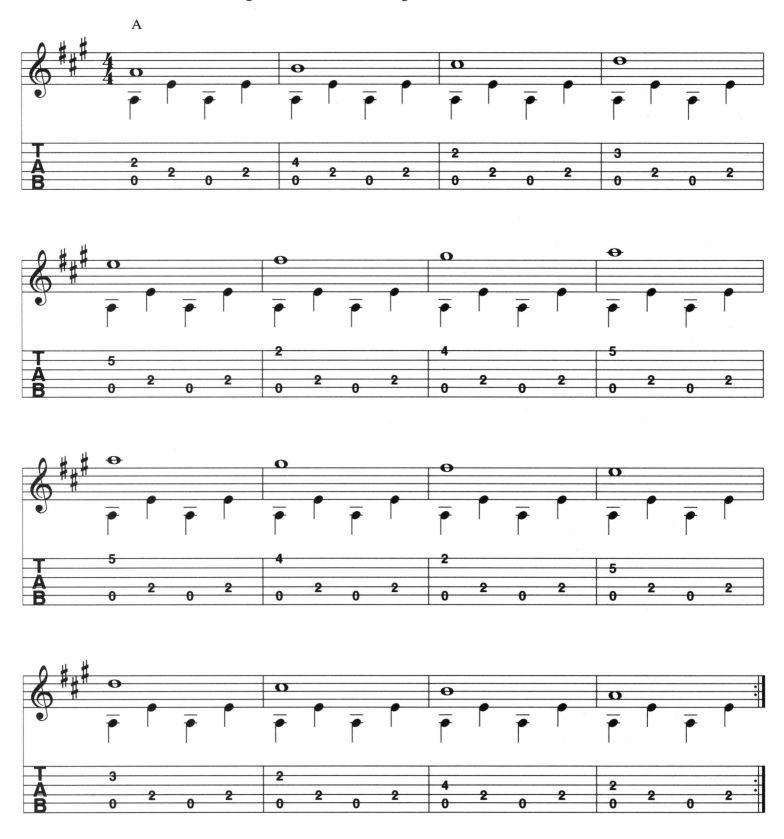

In this exercise play half notes against the alternating bass.

Here we play quarter notes against the alternating bass.

Melody Notes and the D Chord

The following exercises are based on playing the D chord and its related melody notes. Only when the melody note and the chord note conflict must you move your finger off the chord, as in the first measure of the first exercise, where in order to play the melody note G you have to remove your first finger from the chord note A.

Notice the new fingering for the D chord. Playing with the thumb on the low F♯ is a common practice of traditional bluesmen.

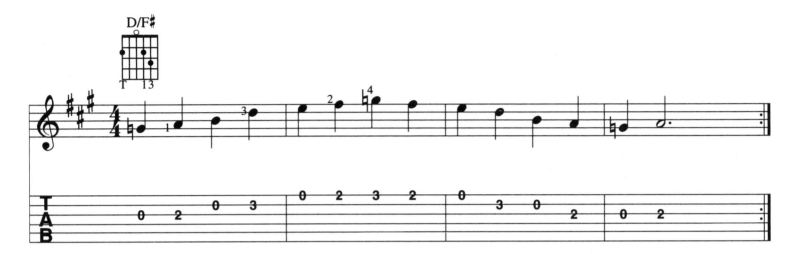

D Chord Melody Notes and the Alternating Bass

In this exercise be sure to hold down the chord as you play the melody notes against the alternating bass.

Also play the D chord and its related scale tones in whole notes and quarter notes against the alternating bass.

Melody Notes and the E Chord

Hold down the E chord as shown while you play the melody notes. Using the second finger to hold down two notes frees your third finger to play others. This is another common technique of blues players.

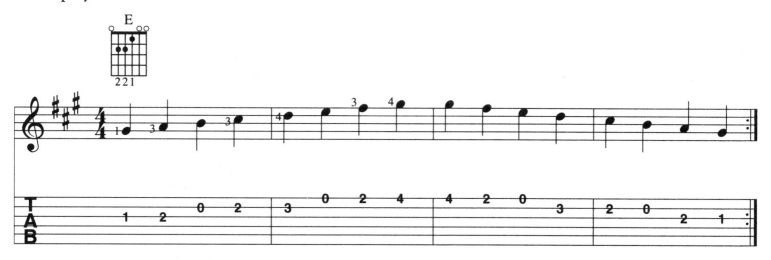

Now, hold down the E chord while playing melody notes against the alternating bass.

For additional practice hold down the E chord while playing the melody notes in whole notes and quarter notes against the alternating bass.

Now that you've practiced playing the melody notes related to the A, D, and E chords, let's play a blues which makes use of all the scale tones in the key of A.

First and Second Endings

Before we play this next blues, look at the *first ending* bar in the eleventh and twelfth measures. The blues is usually played for more than one chorus, and the first ending is a device that indicates that you should return to the beginning of the progression. The first ending is sometimes called a *turnaround* simply because that's what it does; it turns you around to the beginning. Notice that the twelfth measure in the first ending contains an E(V) chord which sets you up harmonically to return to the tonic (A) chord in the first measure. At the second ending you stay on the A chord.

BLUES IN A WITH MELODY NOTES

Melody Notes and the G Chord

Now we will hold down the G chord while playing its related melody notes.

Once again hold down the G chord while playing the melody notes against the alternating bass.

For additional practice hold down the G chord and play the melody notes in whole notes and quarter notes against the alternating bass. Use the same rhythmic figures as with the A chord.

Melody Notes and the C Chord

Hold down the C chord while playing the related melody notes.

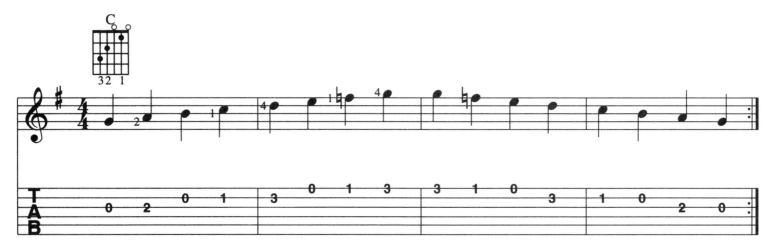

Hold down the C chord throughout the following exercise, which
is based on that chord and its related melody notes, all played
against the alternating bass. It is important that the second finger
of the fretting hand hold down the alternating bass note E as well
as the melody note A. It would be best to use the second finger to
press down both notes. Although such situations don't occur very
often, if a conflict does arise between the melody and the bass,
make the melody sing and keep the rhythm moving by stroking
the muted string with your picking-hand thumb.

Don't forget to play the above exercise with whole notes and
quarter notes too.

Blues in G with Melody Notes

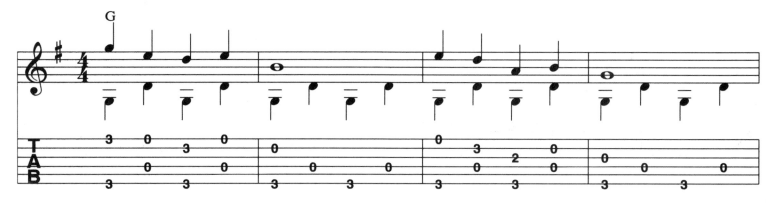

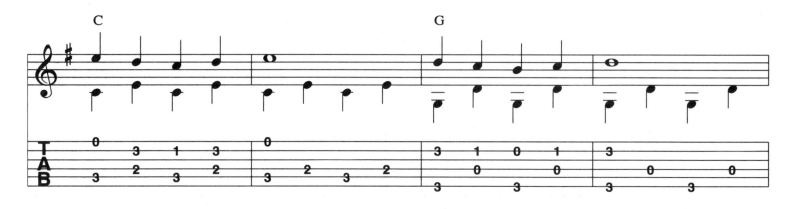

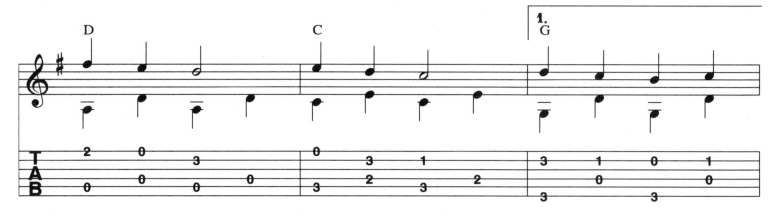

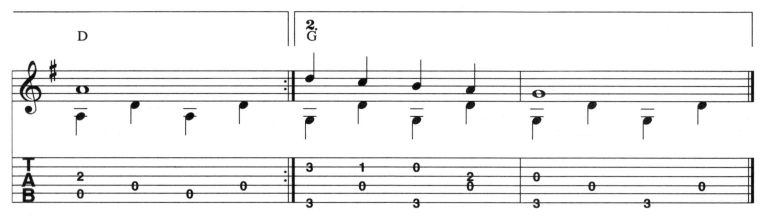

Melody Notes and the B7 Chord

In this exercise hold down the B7 chord as shown and play its
related melody notes.

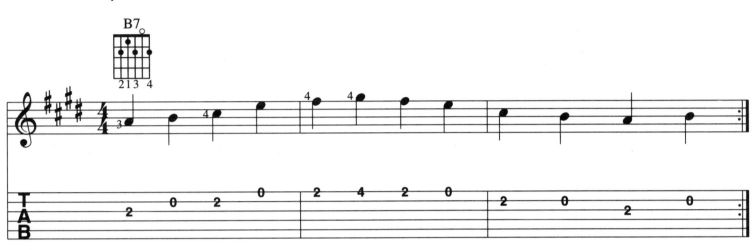

Be sure to hold down the B7 chord throughout the entire exercise
as you play the melody notes against the alternating bass.

Play the above exercise in whole notes and quarter notes against
the alternating bass.

Here is an example of a blues played in the key of E but with tones that are not part of the chords they are played over. An earlier blues played in the key of E (page 20) used only chord tones. The addition of other scale tones adds variety to the tune.

BLUES IN E WITH MELODY NOTES

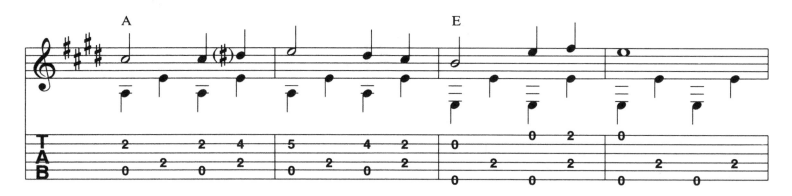

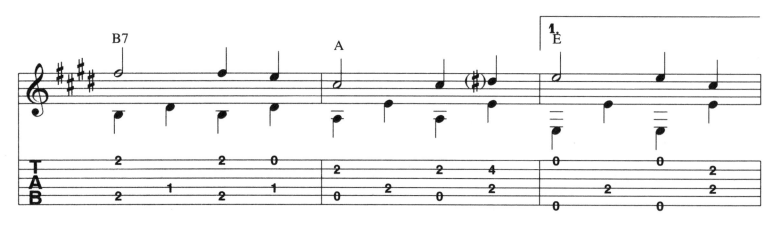

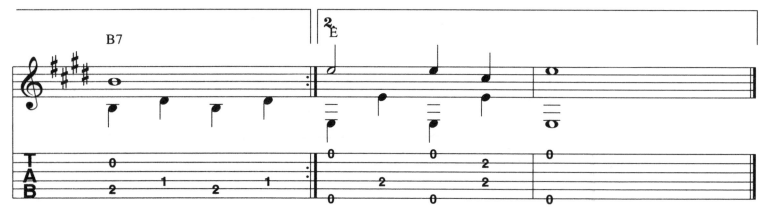

Eighth Notes, Dotted Notes, and Syncopation

This is an eighth note ♪

Two eighth notes are written like this ♫

Two eighth notes equal one quarter note ♫ = ♩

When playing eighth notes it is helpful to tap your foot and count aloud. Play the following exercise and tap your foot. Note that we call the and the *offbeat*.

Eighth Notes and the Alternating Bass

The following exercises are based on playing various combinations of eighth and quarter notes against the quarter-note alternating bass. Be sure your thumb maintains a steady beat. Repeat each exercise as many times as it takes to play smoothly.

This next exercise uses G-chord melody tones in eighth notes against the quarter-note alternating bass. Play slowly and count aloud.

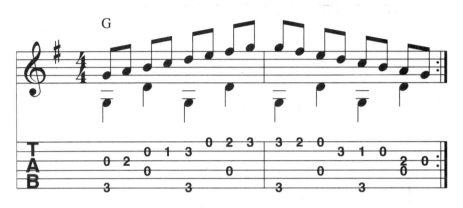

Here are a few more exercises to give you some practice.

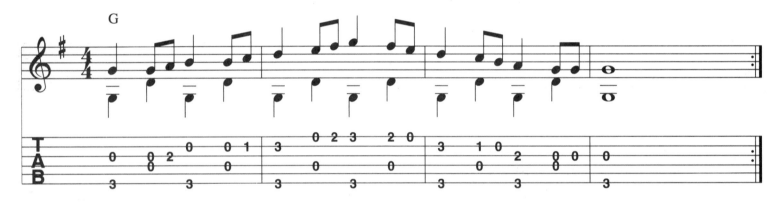

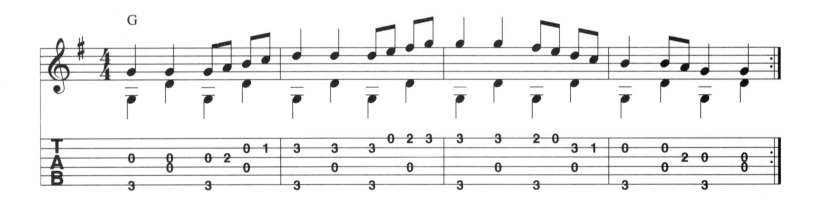

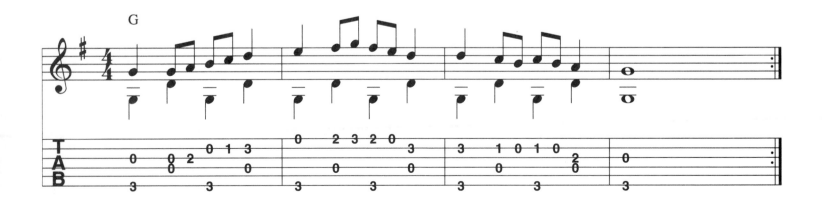

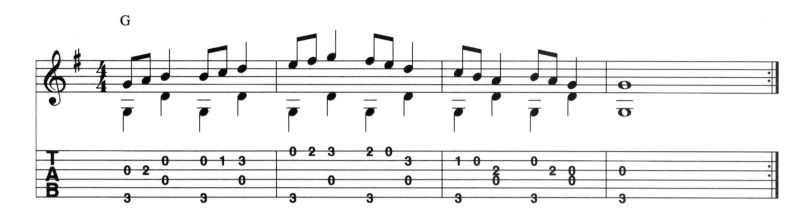

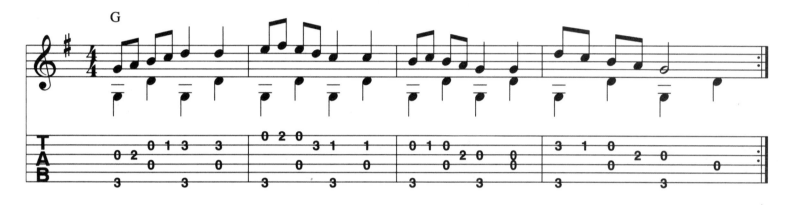

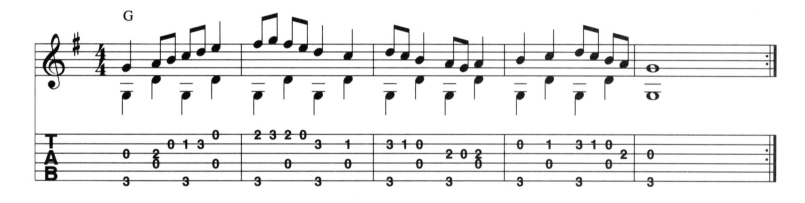

Now let's use some of the rhythms we have seen above in a twelve-bar blues format. Below is a blues in the key of A. Note the use of both chord and non-chord tones.

BLUES IN A WITH MIXED RHYTHMS

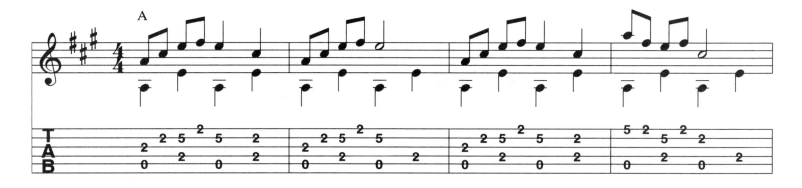

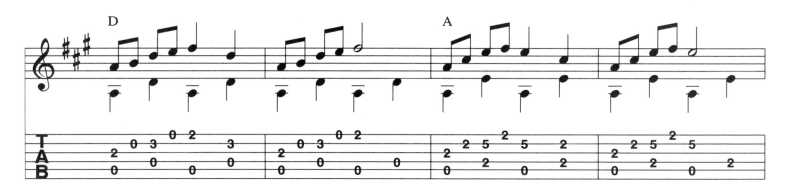

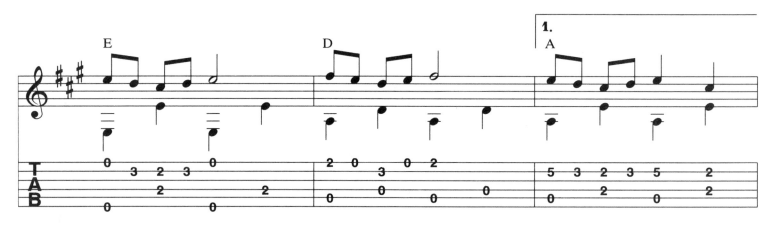

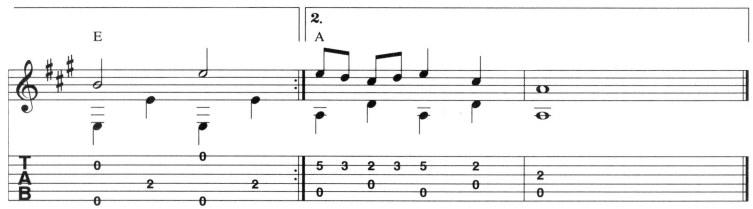

An excellent way of developing your technique is to play the same piece of music in different keys. Here is the same blues you just played but switched to the key of G.

BLUES IN G WITH MIXED RHYTHMS

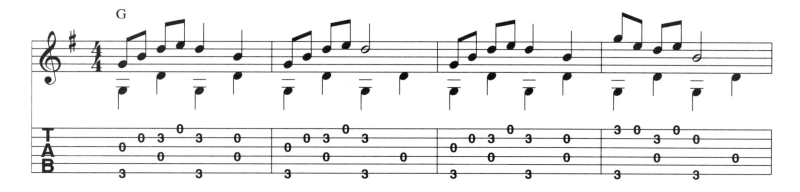

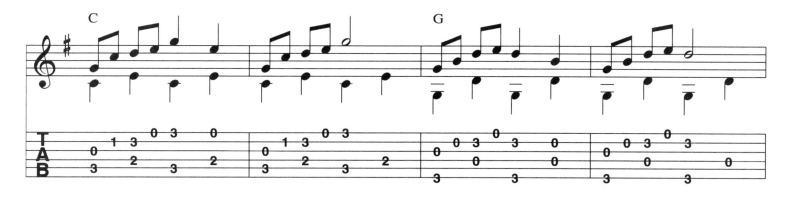

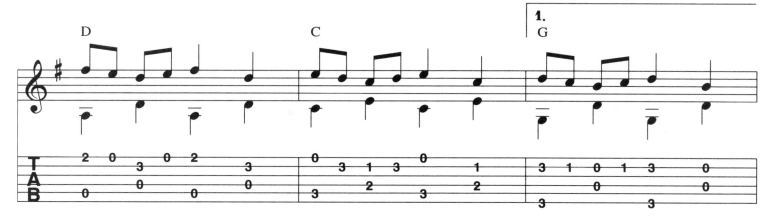

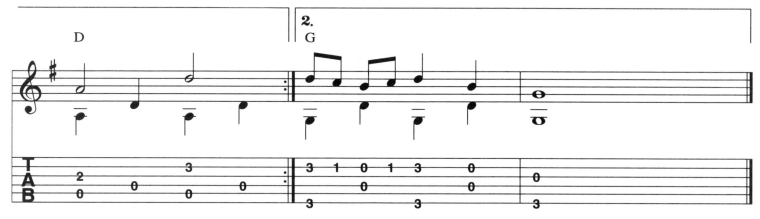

Dotted Rhythms

The Dotted Quarter Note—Eighth Note Combination

The dotted quarter note has a value equal to a quarter note plus an eighth note.

The following exercise illustrates how the dotted quarter note is used. Play slowly and count aloud.

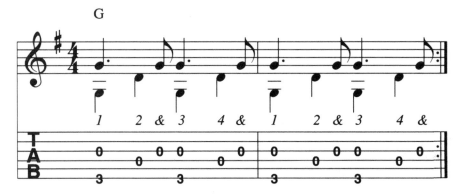

In the following exercise the dotted quarter note is played against a quarter-note alternating bass. It would be most helpful to count this aloud, making sure that the eighth note is played exactly between the two quarter notes in the bass.

This exercise employs scale tones over a G chord.

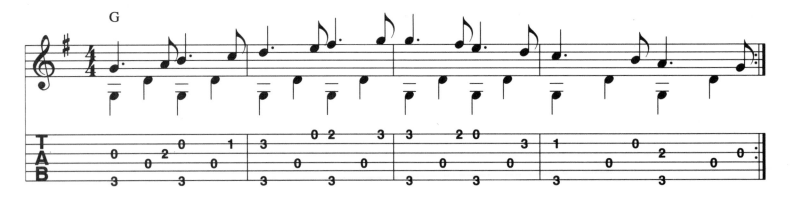

The Eighth Note—Dotted Quarter Note Combination

The following exercise illustrates how the dotted quarter note is played when it follows an eighth note. It's very important that you count aloud while playing through this exercise.

This   *with these ties*   *becomes this*

Here an eighth note—dotted quarter note rhythm is played against the quarter-note alternating bass. Keep counting aloud.

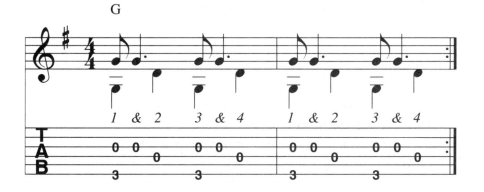

In this exercise the G-chord melody notes are played as eighth notes followed by dotted quarter notes against the quarter-note alternating bass.

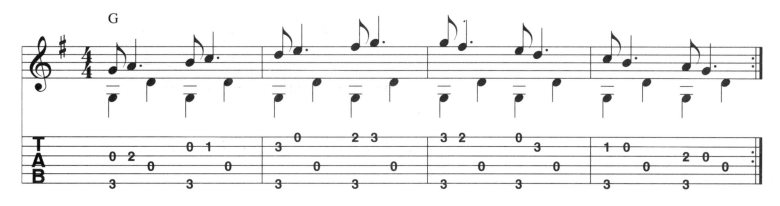

Now we will combine the dotted quarter note–eighth note pattern with an eighth note-dotted quarter note pattern played against an alternating bass.

Now let's play the same rhythm combinations as above with the G chord and its related scale tones.

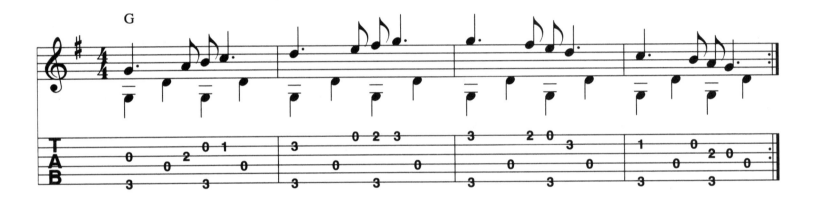

BLUES IN G WITH DOTTED QUARTER NOTES

Syncopation

In blues music containing four beats to the measure there is a natural accent on the first and third beats. These are recognized as strong beats. Syncopation is an intentional shifting of the accent away from these beats, toward the second and fourth beats or the offbeats. Below are several examples of commonly used syncopations.

1 & 2 & 3 & 4 &   *1 & 2 & 3 & 4 &*   *1 & 2 & 3 & 4 &*
  This   *with these ties*   *becomes this*

Notice that two tied eighth notes are written as quarter notes with eighth notes on either side. It's very important that you count this aloud. The accents occur on the offbeats of the second and fourth counts.

Here is the same syncopated figure played against the alternating bass.

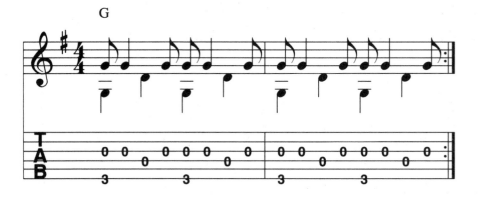

Below are several examples of the use of syncopated figures played against an alternating bass. These examples will be easy to play if you count them aloud and tap your foot on each beat.

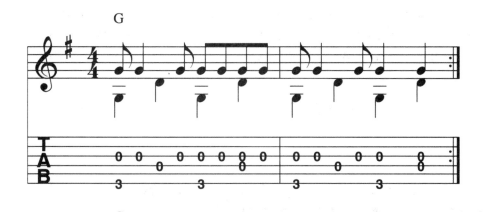

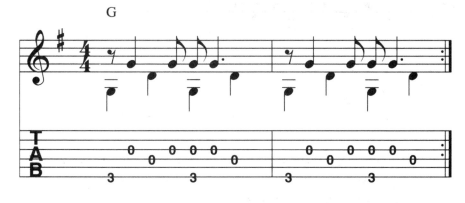

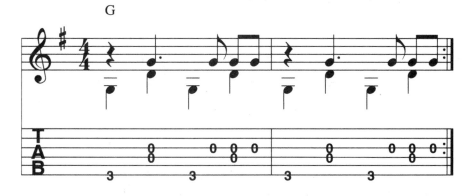

Now let's use some syncopated rhythms in a couple of twelve-bar blues exercises. As always, count along with the alternating bass and try to get a feel for the syncopated rhythms being played against the quarter notes. Pay particular attention to where the & (*and*) comes in between the quarter notes.

BLUES IN G WITH SYNCOPATIONS

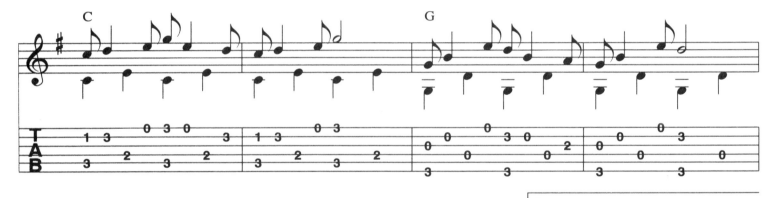

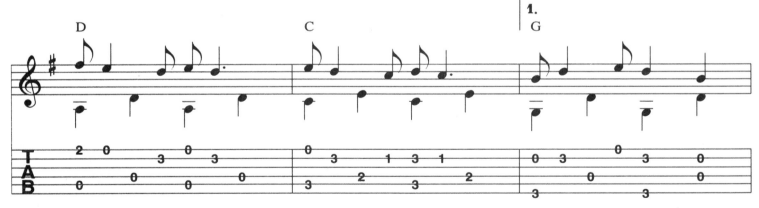

Blues in E with Syncopations

BLUE NOTES

As we discussed earlier, the blues began as a vocal music, but it wasn't long before early jazz bands and jazz instrumentalists began to adopt the form as a vehicle for band arrangements and improvisation. They would try to capture the emotion and the mournful sound of the singing of the blues singer. This sound, so particular to the blues, was a result of the singer's tendency to alter the pitch of certain notes as he sang. These altered notes (which are not in any European scale and, strictly speaking, can only be approximated on a fixed-pitch instrument such as a piano) were heard so often in the blues songs that they came to be called "blue" notes. In trying to imitate the sound of these blues singers jazz instrumentalists began to use these same blue notes in their improvised solos. Let's have a look at them. For our purposes right now, they are the flatted third, fifth, and seventh degrees of the major scale. For example, the blue notes in the key of C are E♭, G♭, and B♭.

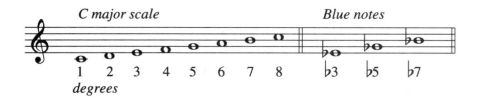

In many of the blues solos which follow you will notice that some of the previously practiced melody notes have become blue notes. These have, through the years, developed into a very important part of every blues player's vocabulary, and are used not only in the blues but also in other forms of music to create a "bluesy" sound. Now our blues pieces will finally begin to leave behind the "straight" major sound of the previous pieces and approach the true blues sound.

This next tune is in the key of E and contains two blue notes associated with that key—G♮ and D♮ (in straight E they would be G♯ and D♯). Although B♭ is also a blue note in the key of E, it is not used in this solo. You do not have to use all the blue notes in any particular tune—or for that matter, any blue notes at all. But they do add a distinctive touch to the music.

Blues in E with Blue Notes

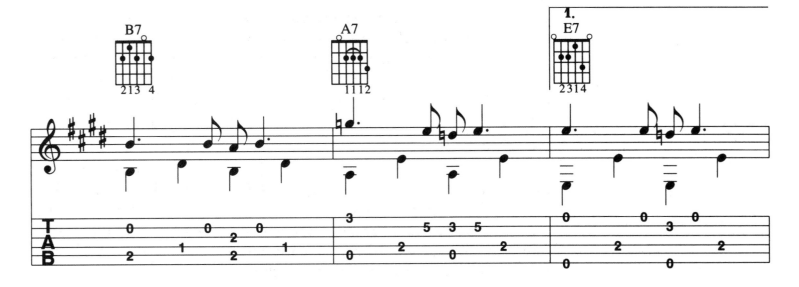

Here is a blues solo in the key of A, including that key's blue notes C♮ and G♮.

Blues in A with Blue Notes

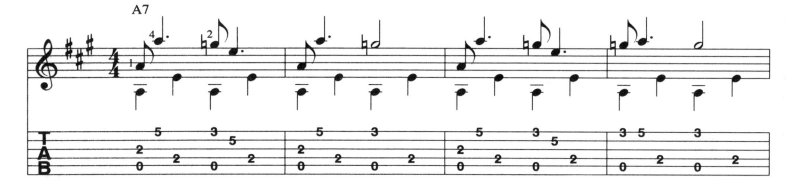

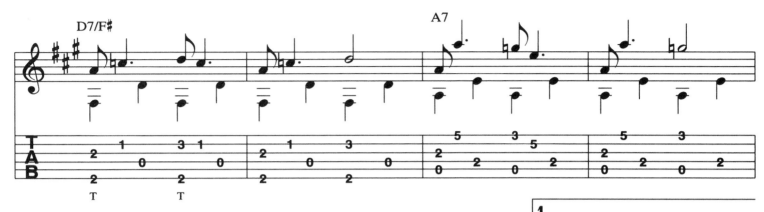

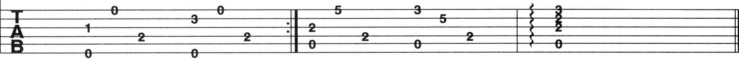

Fretting-Hand Techniques

This chapter is designed to acquaint you with some of the guitaristic techniques found in blues playing. We will examine the use of hammerons and pulloffs, slides, double stops, bends, and vibrato. It is through the use of these techniques that players add individual expression to their blues. These musical nuances are developed over the course of a player's lifetime and are part of what eventually becomes an identifiable style. As we examine each of them listen carefully to the instruction CD to ensure correct interpretation.

Hammerons

A guitarist executes a hammeron by tapping his finger rapidly and cleanly onto the fingerboard to sound a note, as opposed to picking an already held note. A hammeron is most often executed one, two, or three frets (on the same string) above either an open string or a note that has just been picked in the conventional manner.

The first example below shows a hammeron on the offbeat. Simply pick the open G string and then on the offbeat hammer your index finger onto the first fret (G♯).

In our next example we will add an alternating bass. Simply hold an E chord and each time you pick the open G also pick the bass note.

Below we see how the hammeron is incorporated into a musical passage. Again, hold the E7 chord throughout the entire exercise.

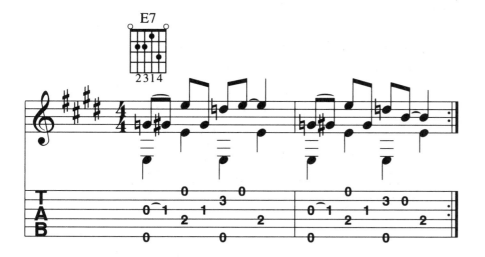

Now let's take a look at a hammeron played on the beat. The example below shows the basic technique. Be sure to count so you can make sure that the hammered note sounds on the first, second, third, and fourth counts of the measure.

And here is a similar hammeron used in a musical passage.

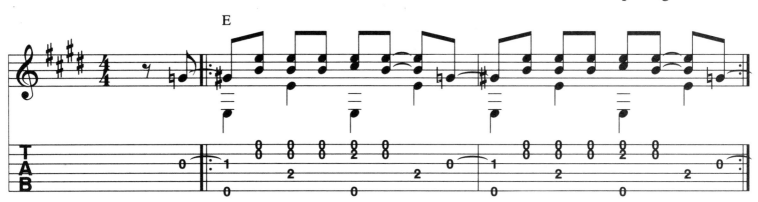

Pulloffs

A pulloff is the opposite of a hammeron; you sound a note by snapping your fretting finger off a held note to let a lower note sound on the same string. In the example below you pick the F♯ on the second fret of the first string and then pull off your finger to sound the open string.

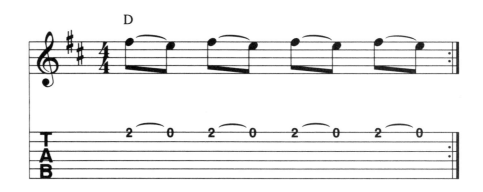

Now let's see how pulloffs can be used in a musical passage. For the next two examples tune the low E string down to D and finger the D chord. In the example below the pulled-off note comes on the offbeat. Pick the F♯ on the first beat while simultaneously striking the bass note D with your thumb. Then, on the offbeat, pull your finger off the F♯ to sound the open E.

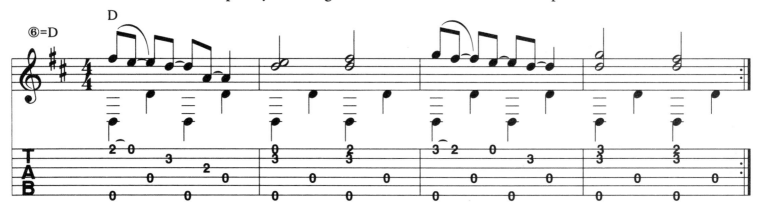

In this example the pulloffs fall both on the beats and on the offbeats. For the pulloff on the beat pick the F♯ on the offbeat and, as the thumb strikes the open D bass note on the beat of the second count, pull off the second finger from the F♯ to sound the open E.

Slides

To play the slides shown below, pick the A on the 3rd string, 2nd fret, then slide up to the 4th fret. Don't pick the second note. Make sure to keep your timing accurate.

In the next example we'll add a bass note, E, to the overall sound. Listen to the accompanying CD.

This example illustrates the chord slide. Note that this slide sounds from the *and* of the fourth count in the first measure to the first beat of the second measure. To execute it play the notes C and G♯ on the first fret with the index finger, then slide this finger up to the second fret just as the thumb strikes the bass note A. Notice the hammeron coming into the first measure.

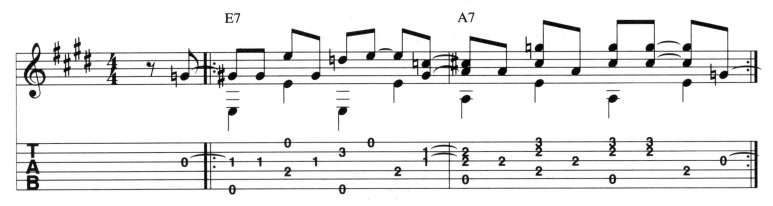

Double Stops

In the simplest sense a double stop means that you play two notes at once. The example below shows a typical blues double stop in the key of E. Notice the high position.

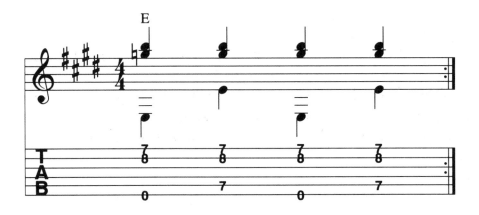

Bends

Perhaps more than any other technique, the bend offers opportunity for expression and nuance. Mastering the art of bending strings can take many years, so have patience. In our first example pick the third fret, first string G and then push the string up towards you. This will raise the pitch of the note. The new note will sound somewhere between a G♮ and a G♯ (i.e., it will be a blue note). Listen to the accompanying CD to hear how it should sound. In the pieces at the end of the book you'll be seeing some bends of this type. We have notated them with a little curved line (‿) coming off the note that is to be bent.

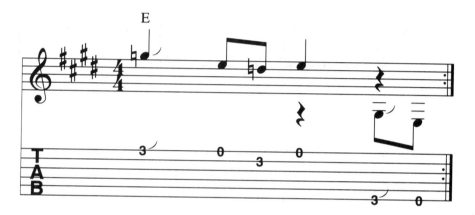

Vibrato

Vibrato refers to the sound produced when you move your finger side-to-side or up-and-down on a string. It's like executing a rapid succession of small bends. The vibrato is controlled by how much and how fast you move your finger on the string. Listen to the accompanying CD to hear the different types of possible vibrato effects.

Picking-Hand Techniques

Up to this point we have studied how to play an alternating bass with the thumb while picking single-note melodies with the fingers. Now we are going to look at a few other techniques that will help our playing sound even more authentic.

The Brushstroke

The brushstroke gives a nice rhythmic drive to any blues accompaniment and provides a simple, effective contrast to the single-note picking we've been using. In the first example we see the brushstroke used with an E chord. The alternating bass is simply an E in octaves. The stroke is executed by brushing your index finger up against the three top strings. The brushstrokes are played on the offbeats, while the alternating bass is always played on the beat. Be sure to hold the E chord throughout the exercise.

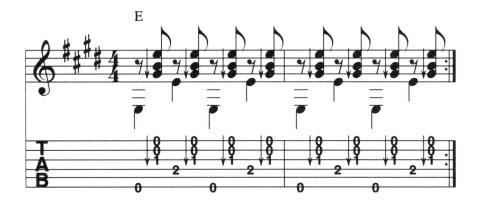

Now try a brushstroke and alternating bass for the A7 chord.

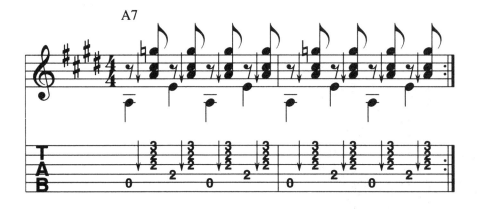

And here is a brushstroke with the B7 chord.

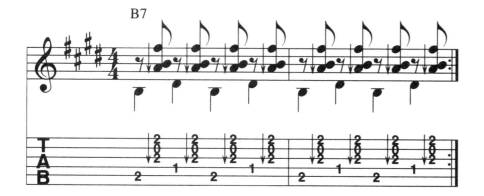

At this point try going back and playing through some blues progressions using the brushstroke technique. Only by constantly playing these new techniques through blues progressions in different keys will you gain facility in using them.

Heel Damping

Heel damping is one of the most useful tools in a guitar player's picking-hand approach. It can help to separate the bass from the treble and tighten the overall sound of the guitar. It can also be used to muffle just the bass strings, giving the thumbed notes a more percussive attack. When used skillfully in combination with undamped treble strings it can create the illusion of two guitarists playing together.

Rest the heel of your picking hand on top of the strings right next to the bridge of the guitar. By experimenting you will be able to find the position that will be most comfortable for you. The most important thing is to achieve the desired sound while avoiding any unnecessary tension in your hand. Look at the pictures for the correct position and listen to the CD for the sound. (The CD will illustrate the example below with and without heel damping.) It will take a lot of practice to master this technique, so stay with it. A good idea would be to go back to some of the earlier exercises in the book and play them with heel damping.

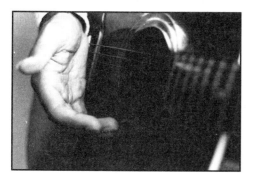

Walking Basslines

Walking basslines work very well with heel damping and brushstroking. A walking bassline is constructed from the notes of the chord. Let's take the key of G and examine this technique. The example below shows a bassline for the G chord. Strike the bass notes with your thumb while brushing up with the the index finger on the offbeats. Pay particular attention to the fretting-hand fingering indications.

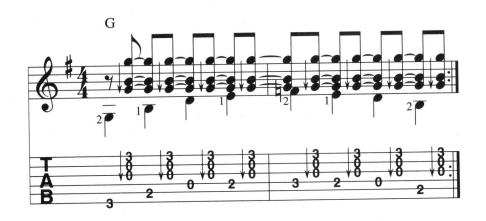

Here is a walking bassline for the C chord.

And here is a walking bassline for the D chord.

Now let's combine the above three chords into a twelve-bar blues in the key of G. The following tune sounds similar to what Blind Boy Fuller played in his "Step It Up And Go" blues.

BLUES IN G WITH WALKING BASS

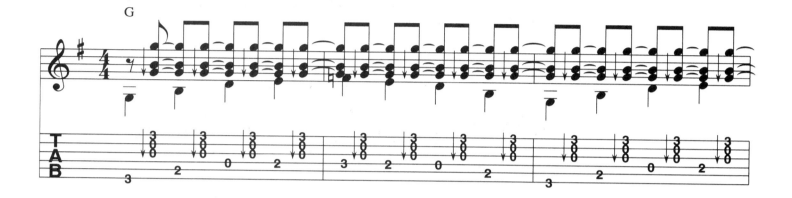

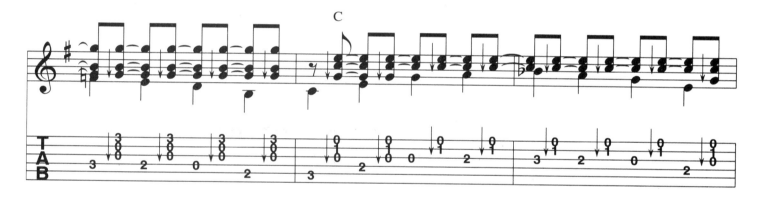

The positions required to execute the bassline in the key of E are fairly difficult. If you can't manage them now come back to this section when you have developed more strength in your fretting hand. The bassline for the E chord requires a lot of work with the little finger. Try the alternate fingering for the E chord to help you reach the G♯ and C♯ with the pinky. Below is a picture of this fingering with the little finger reaching the G♯.

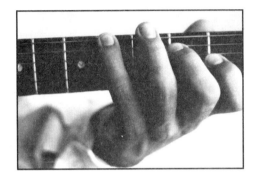

Here is a walking bassline for the E chord.

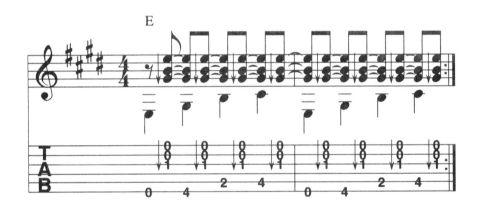

The next example shows a bassline for the A chord. Use your index finger to hold down all three of the notes on the second fret. Reach up for the C♯ and F♯ notes with your ring finger.

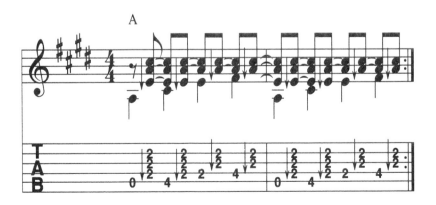

For the B7 chord use the alternating bass that we looked at earlier.

Now let's play a twelve-bar blues in E with a walking bassline. Listen to the CD to hear how effective this style can be as an accompaniment pattern. Try it with and without heel damping.

Blues in E with Walking Bass

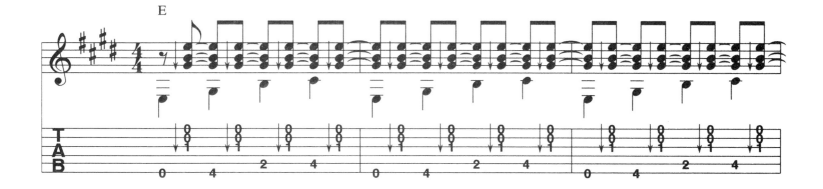

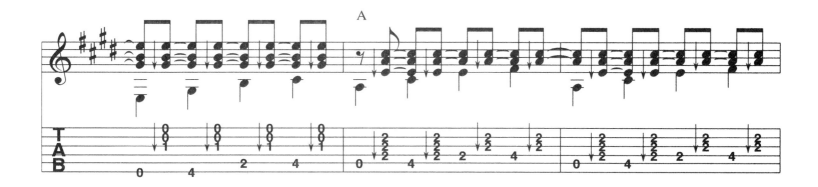

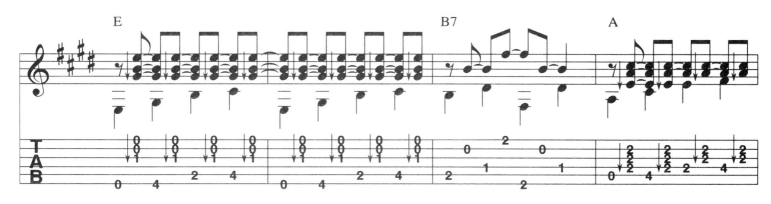

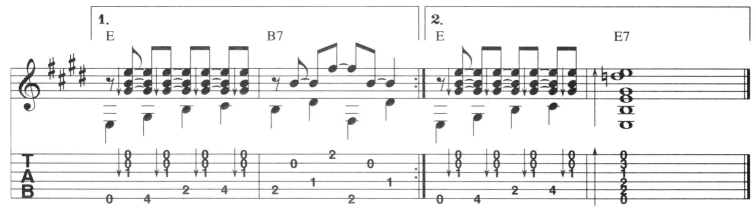

Playing Chords in the Higher Positions

Up to this point most of the chords we've been using have been played in the open position on the lowest region of the fingerboard. Now we're going to see how it is possible to play some of them higher up. Doing so will enable us to pull off some much more sophisticated blues. For our first example, let's use the E7 chord. Here it is in the basic open position.

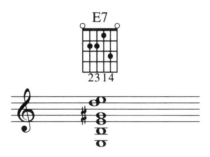

Below is the same chord played in IInd, Vth, and IXth positions. (The position refers to the resting point of the first finger along the fretboard.)

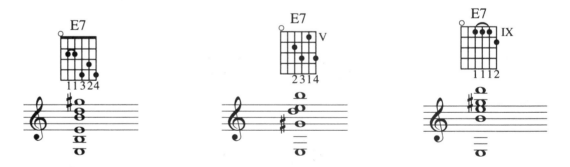

The exercise on the next page is based on the four different positions of the E7 chord shown above. Strike each chord four times in each measure. Be sure to play from chord to chord as smoothly as possible. Try different combinations.

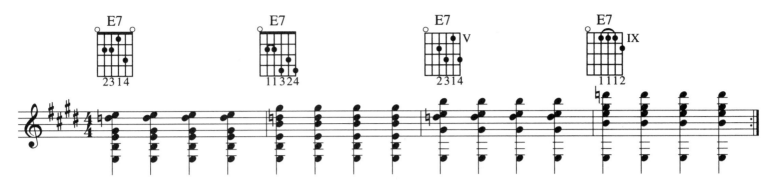

Now let's look at some of the different positions available for the A7 chord. Here is the basic open-position A7 chord.

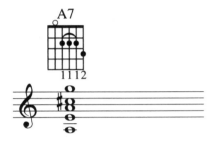

Below is the A7 chord shown in three different positions.

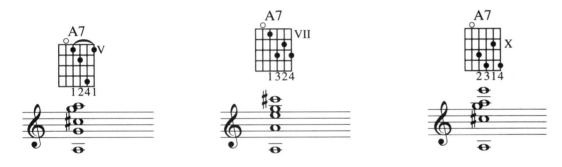

The following exercise is based on the A7 chord played in the various positions shown above. Again, try different combinations of the positions.

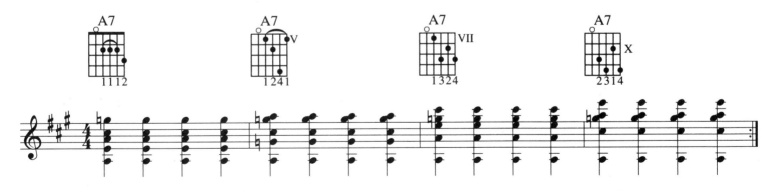

Now let's look at the B7 chord with a few of its possible position forms. Here is the open-position form that you should know well by now.

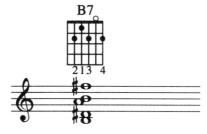

And here are some different positions for it.

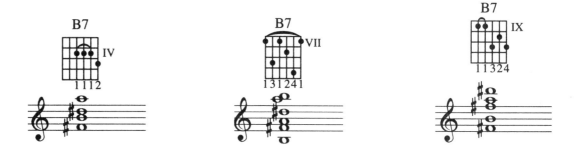

This next exercise is based on the B7 chord and its different positions. Once again, try to play all the changes as smoothly as possible.

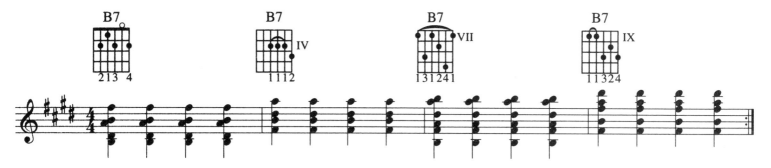

In order to create a more "bluesy" feeling, many players voice all their chords as seventh chords. We've just learned how to play different inversions of the E7, A7, and B7 chords. As you know, these chords are the primary chords in the key of E. Before we play a blues solo with them let's first practice moving smoothly among them. Below are three exercises based on the E7, A7, and B7 chords using the new voicings we've just learned.

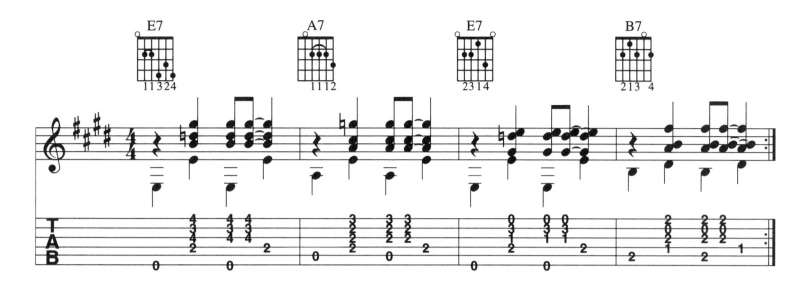

This next example uses only higher-position chords.

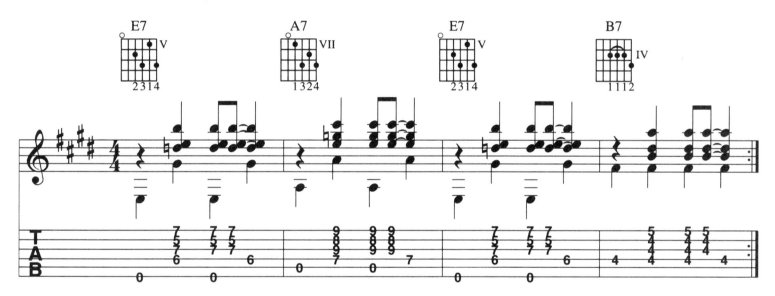

And now we'll try descending through the chord inversions.

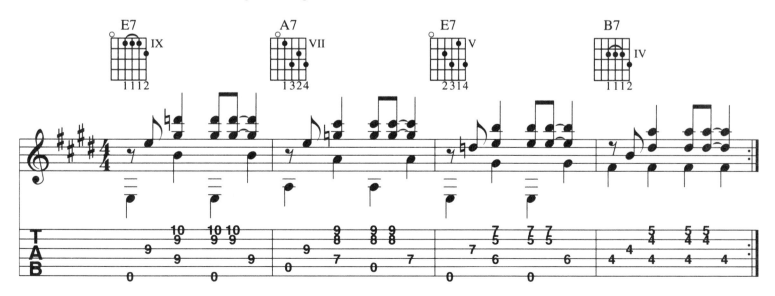

And finally, here's a blues using seventh chords in a variety of positions. Watch for slight variations.

BLUES IN E WITH SEVENTHS AND INVERSIONS

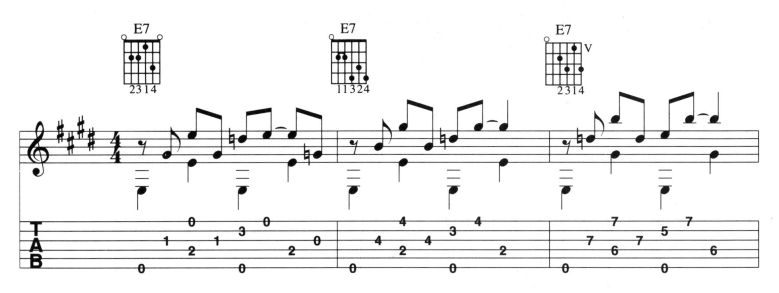

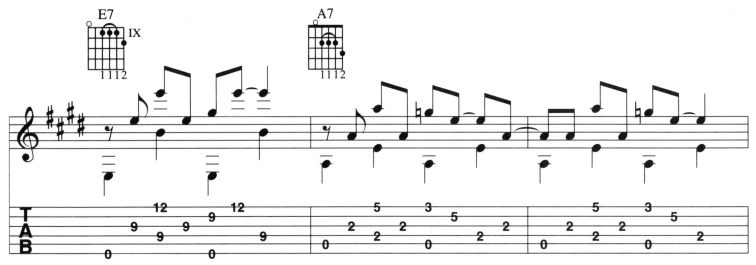

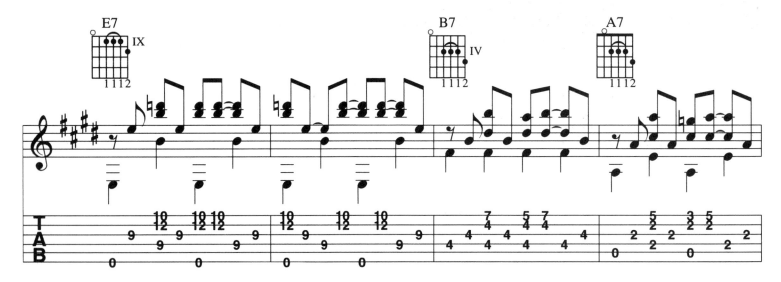

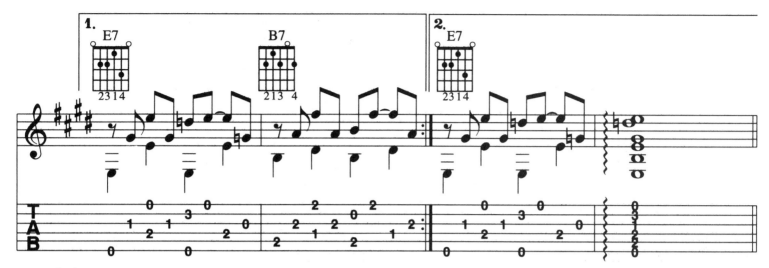

second chorus

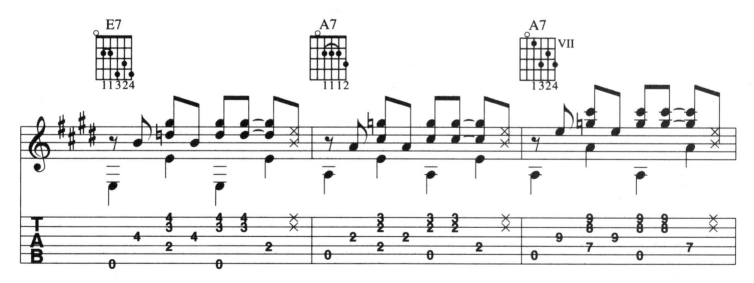

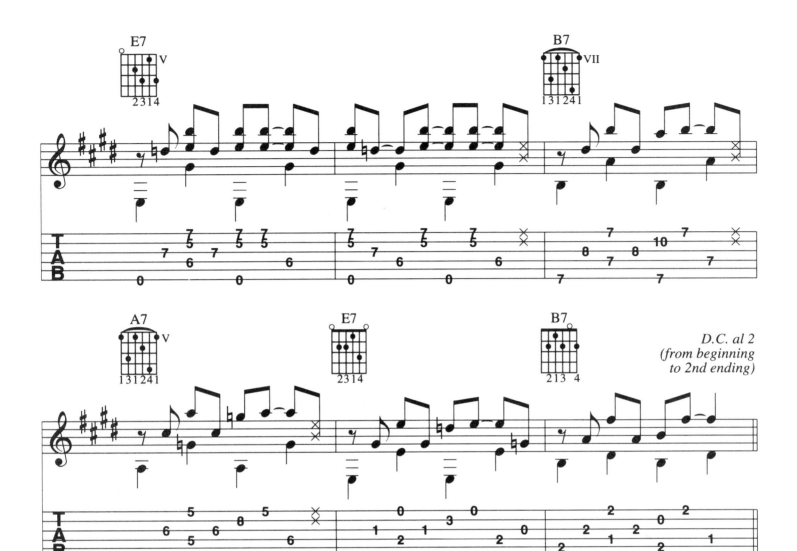

Next we'll try a blues in the key of G using seventh and ninth chords. We'll be trying out some new chord forms. The diagrams and the tab will clue you in to the right fingerings. Ninth chords are just seventh chords with an extra tone a third above the seventh.

BLUES IN G WITH SEVENTHS AND INVERSIONS

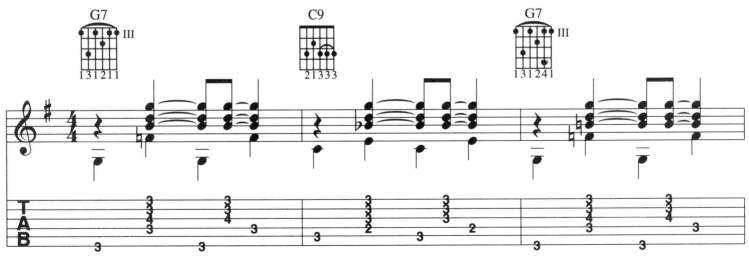

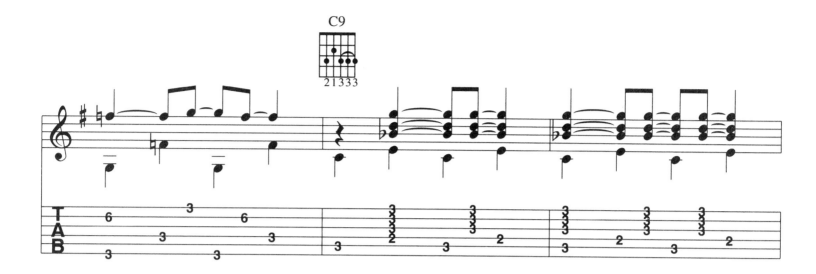

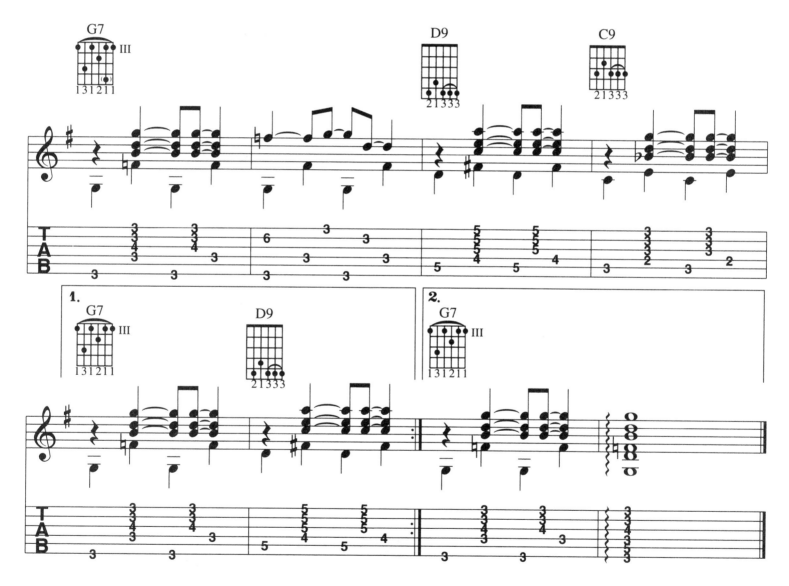

VAMPS

In order to establish a particular mood, a blues player will often play a short phrase or riff over and over again before starting his piece. Such a phrase is known as a *vamp*. Vamps are also used as segues between short pieces in the same key. Below is an example of a vamp in the key of C. Note that we are using a relatively complex bassline. To execute it simply alternate your fretting-hand ring finger between the low C and G notes. Practice the vamp until you can play it smoothly and with a flowing rhythmic feeling.

Now let's play a series of short pieces which we will connect by using the above vamp. These five pieces are typical of the "sweet" country blues style associated with such players as Mississippi John Hurt and Etta Baker.

Use the vamp you've just practiced as an introduction to the first piece. When you've finished, go back into the vamp to connect you with the second piece. Notice that these pieces are not the usual blues that we've been playing. They are not twelve bars in length and do not use the usual chord progression.

PIECE #1

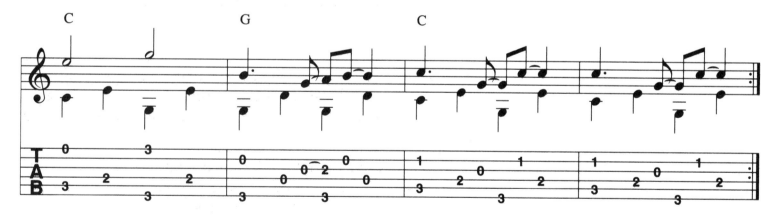

Piece #2

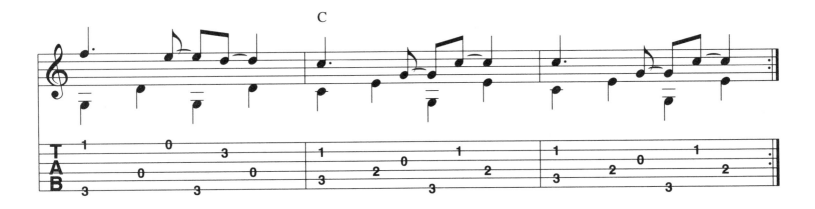

Piece #3

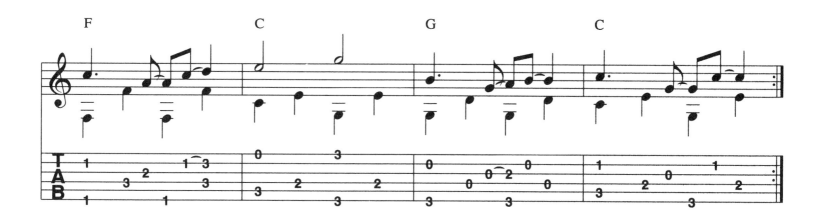

For the next segment we've written out two bars of the vamp in order to show that the note on the offbeat of the fourth count in the second measure of the vamp has been changed to a high G (1st string, 3rd fret) so that it will move smoothly into the first beat of the piece. Thus the G on the first count of the piece is anticipated in the vamp. Notice also that there is a chord change on the third count of the second measure.

Piece #4

Finally, we'll move into a short piece by veteran blues player Etta Baker. Note the tension she creates by using some rather odd intervals. Don't be misled by the dissonant-sounding notes on the first count of the first measure. To produce these notes simply move an E7 chord shape up one fret on the fingerboard.

Piece #5

Here are two more vamps that can be used as intros to any blues
in the key of E.

VAMP IN E #1

VAMP IN E #2

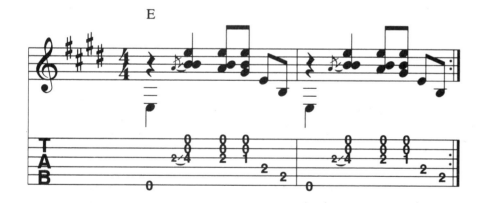

SINGING THE BLUES

The most powerful and direct manner of expressing the blues is by singing. The earliest blues grew out of work songs, church songs, chants, and field hollers, and were sung unaccompanied. The guitar became the logical choice for an accompanying instrument, as it was relatively inexpensive, portable, and offered both rhythmic and harmonic capabilities. With this in mind let us examine the basic relationship between blues singing and the guitar accompaniment.

The Blues Lyric Form

The most commonly used form of the blues, as we've already discussed, is the twelve-bar form. The blues lyric divides these twelve bars into three sections taking up four bars each:

A *(opening statement)*   I got these blues, Mama, I'm not satisfied.

A *(repeat of statement)*   I got these blues, Mama, I'm not satisfied.

B *(answering statement)*   Well, that's the reason I ran away and cried.

The music below shows how the lyrics fall across the twelve bars. In this tune each four-bar phrase starts on the *and* of the fourth count. *Pickup notes* like these are common in blues lyrics.

Now let's take a closer look at each of the above three sections. Notice that within each four-bar section the lyric part occupies only two bars and is followed by a pause. It is in this two-bar pause that the guitarist has an opportunity to fill in with a short solo or riff. This is the "call-and-response." The singer sings, or "calls," for two bars and the guitar "responds" for two bars. The music below illustrates a complete blues arrangement, beginning with a two-bar vamp taken from the last chapter.

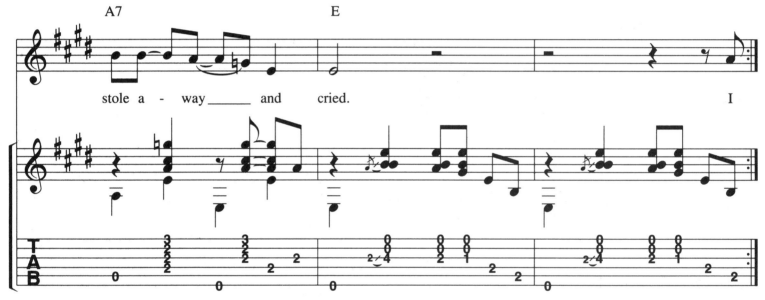

Below are three fills or responses that could have been used in the blues just played. Learn each one and then go back and play the blues arrangement using it in the response part. There are an infinite number of possible fills. Try to make up your own using these as starting points.

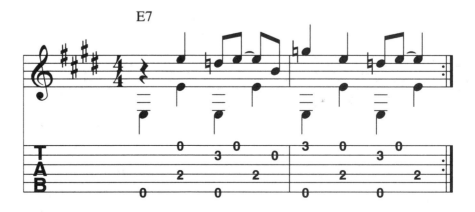

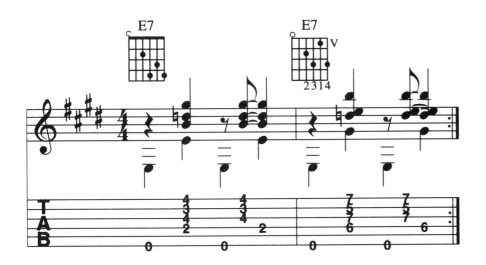

This next fill is played on the upper register of the fingerboard.

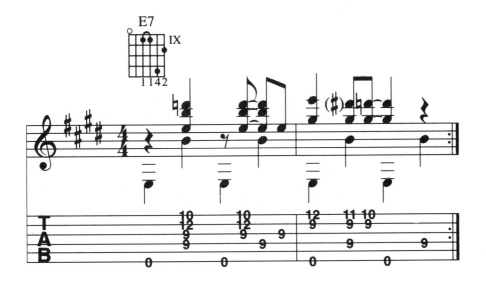

Turnaround Fills

We have already discussed how a blues can be repeated as many times as the player wants. Each time the blues is to be repeated a turnaround is used in the eleventh and twelfth measures. Below are three examples of turnaround fills which may be played in those measures and are designed to lead you back to the beginning of the progression. After you get the idea try to make up some of your own.

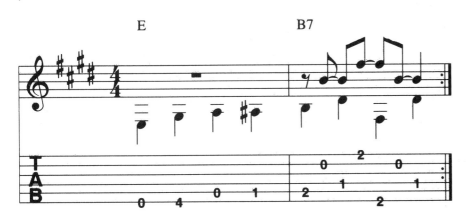

At this point you should have some idea of how to approach singing a blues, and of the possible interplay between the voice and the guitar. Try making up your own blues lyric using the A-A-B pattern we discussed on page 76. Then add an accompaniment and fills and you will have a song!

Five Blues Pieces

We will conclude with five complete blues pieces. Four of them are arrangements of traditional songs, and the fifth is an original instrumental. The pieces were selected for their musical as well as their educational value. Each contains techniques we have already studied, but here we are more concerned with them as types of authentic blues than as exercises.

These arrangements should be starting points for your own experience with this music. In order to fully appreciate them, as well as to understand what goes into interpreting and arranging blues songs, you should listen to the original artists and hear how they played. Please consult the discography for details on recordings of the songs.

At this point the compact disc will be your best guide. Use the written music as a road map to understand chord positions and frets. We have included a written analysis of each piece, but the bulk of the explanations appear on the CD, which will take you through each tune step-by-step. We can't stress too much that the best way to learn this kind of music is to listen to the recordings of the greats.

M & O Blues

This Mississippi Delta blues, popularized by the great Willie Brown, is a highly rhythmic piece. Although it is written here in the key of E, it was played on the recording with a capo on the second fret. After you've learned the piece as written, play it with the capo. Either of the two sections can be used as an accompaniment for the vocal, but the second section will also work well as an instrumental. Start by learning the first section, as it is much easier. The second section will require careful listening to the CD to ensure correct interpretation.

Musical Analysis
If you have studied the section on fretting-hand techniques on pages 50-55, the music in the first section should present no problem. Indeed, the last hammeron example (page 54) from that section was designed specifically to prepare you for this piece. You might also try playing the tune using the brushstroke technique.

Section two of "M & O Blues" is built primarily around an extended melodic phrase, contrasting with the rhythmic playing of section one. Hear how effective this melodic phrase is as an accompaniment to the vocal. After you've learned this part of the tune you can begin to add the vocal line over the instrumental.

Vocal melody

M&O BLUES

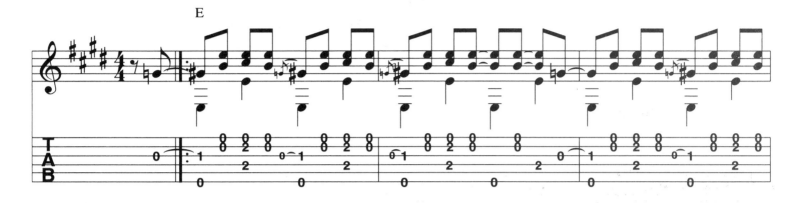

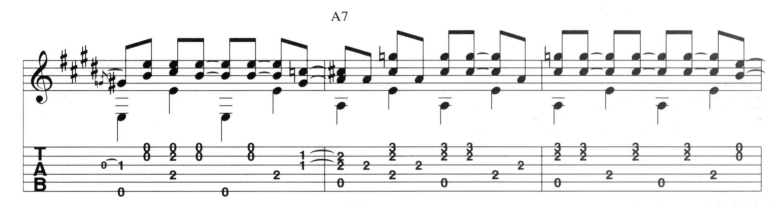

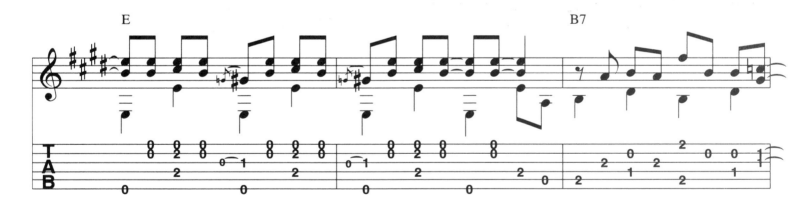

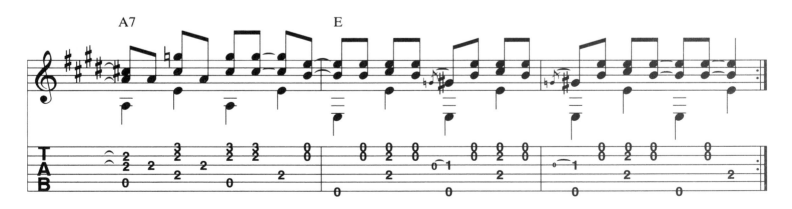

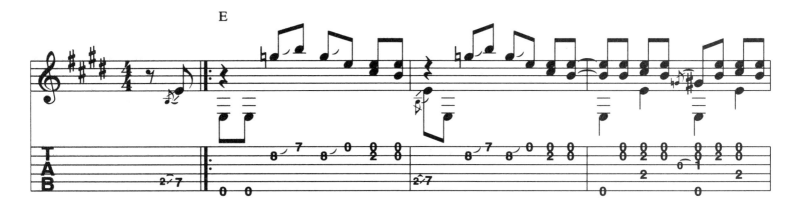

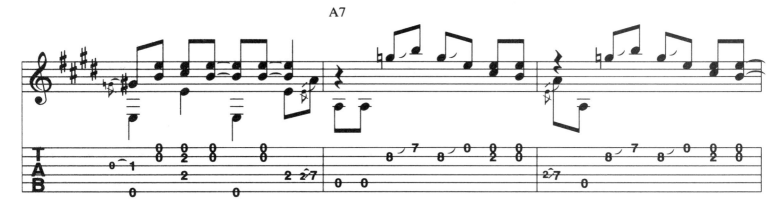

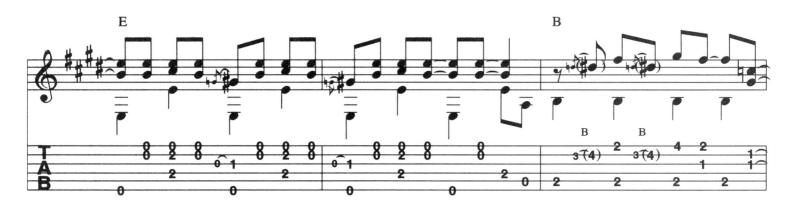

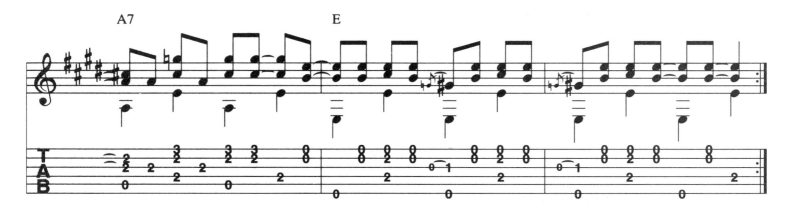

Additional lyrics

2. I got a notion and, Lord, I believe that I will.

   I got a notion and, Lord, I believe that I will.

   I'm gonna build me a mansion out on Decatur Hill.

3. I asked her how 'bout it, and Lordy, she said "alright."

   I asked her how 'bout it, and Lordy, she said "alright."

   But then she never showed up at the shack last night.

4. I started to beat my woman 'til she laid down 'cross my bed

   I started to beat my woman 'til she laid down 'cross my bed.

   But then she looked so ambitious I took back all the words I said.

5. *Repeat first verse*

BEEKMAN BLUES

This original instrumental is the first of two pieces that use a drop-D tuning. The title comes from the town of Beekman, New York, where there is a two-hundred-year-old roadhouse that has long been a gathering place for musicians. It was there that Mark Galbo first saw Taj Mahal; this piece is highly influenced by Mahal's playing.

Musical Analysis

The piece has been arranged in two parts. The first is a straightforward alternating bass with hammerons and pulloffs. This should present no problems if you've studied those moves in the section on fretting-hand techniques (page 54). Notice that in measure six, on the offbeat of the fourth count, we return to the D chord, anticipating the next measure by a half beat.

The second part is just an eight-bar solo idea that you can substitute for the first eight bars of part one. The last four bars remain unchanged. Notice that this part is written as four bars with a repeat. To execute the solo simply come out of the D chord and slide your ring finger up the B string (2nd) to the 7th fret. To get the correct interpretation listen to the CD. Below is a picture of the higher position that you will slide to.

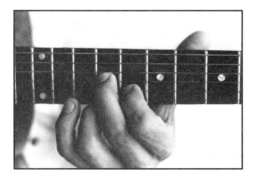

BEEKMAN BLUES

Tune 6th string to D

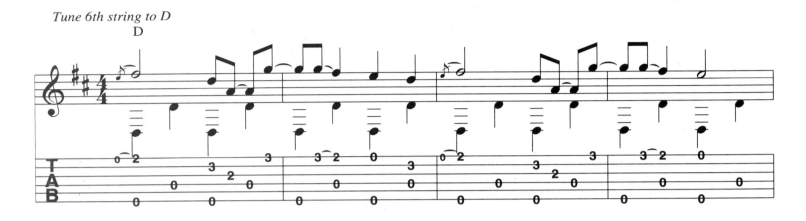

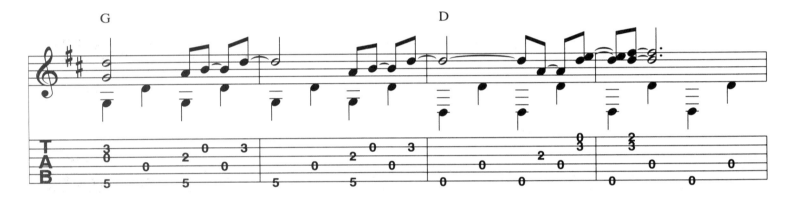

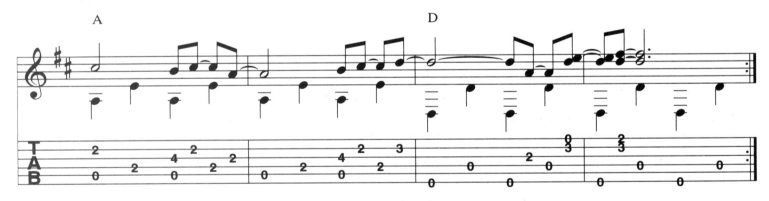

BIG ROAD BLUES

This is a Mississippi Delta-style piece derived from the playing of Tommy Johnson. It is played, like "Beekman Blues," in drop-D tuning, and features a classic octave bassline. For a great listening experience you should try to hear the original recording: Johnson had a truly unique vocal style.

Musical Analysis

The piece has been arranged with a vamp intro, alternating between D major and D minor chords. Master this pattern before going on to the rest of the piece, since it is the structure on which everything else is built. As you listen to the CD you will hear that the vocal can be delivered over either the vamp or the octave bassline. The bassline is best executed by using the thumb on the lower note and snapping the higher note on the D string with the index finger. Practice this part separately until it you have mastered it. Then add the treble double stops found in the bass lead riff. Notice that you pinch these treble notes in combination with the bass note. Keep the bassline moving without interruption, as it is a very effective part of the piece and gives the illusion of two guitars playing at once.

Notice in the eighth measure that on the *and* of the fourth count there is an open A note. Hit this note with your thumb and then in measure five immediately hit a B on the first beat, again with your thumb. On the *and* of the fourth count of measure eight start a chord slide into the A chord of measure nine. We discussed this in our section on fretting-hand techniques (page 54).

Big Road Blues

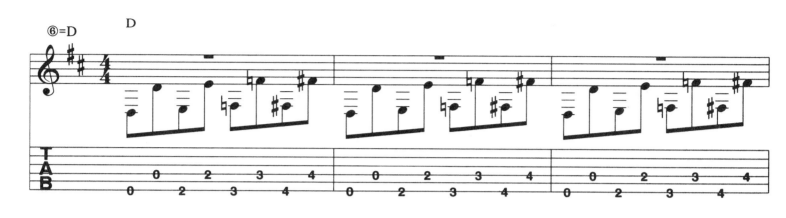

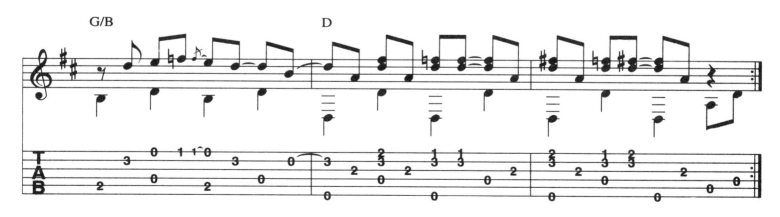

Additional lyrics

2. Now the Mississippi River, it's so deep and wide.

Now the Mississippi River, it's so deep and wide.

Now I be so worried, baby, tryin' to cross to the other side.

3. Cryin', sun's gonna shine, baby, through my door someday.

Cryin', sun's gonna shine, baby, through my door someday.

Well this rain's gonna change, gonna blow these blues away.

4. *Repeat first verse*

32-20 BLUES

This is another Delta blues by the legendary Robert Johnson. It is in the key of A, a very popular key for blues players because of all the open strings that it makes available. The drone bass used during the first four measures gives the piece a special driving quality. The title refers to a type of sawed-off shotgun, which should help you to understand the lyrics better!

Musical Analysis

"32-20 Blues" contains a good example of the famous Robert Johnson turnaround. We see it during the introduction as well as at the end. Note the descending melodic line on the 4th string (in the third measure of the intro and elsewhere). Be sure to listen to the CD and examine the photographs. Although the turnaround may be difficult at first, stay with it. It will get easier with practice.

On the D9 chord (fourth measure of the verse) use a thumbstroke on beat two and a brushstroke on the *and* of three. Notice also the brushstroking in bars 1-4, 7, and 8.

32-20 BLUES

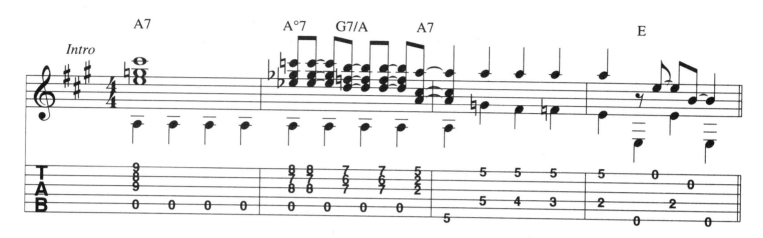

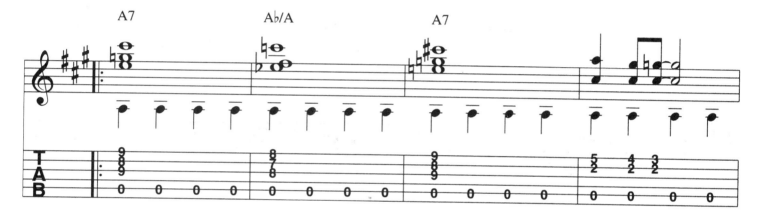

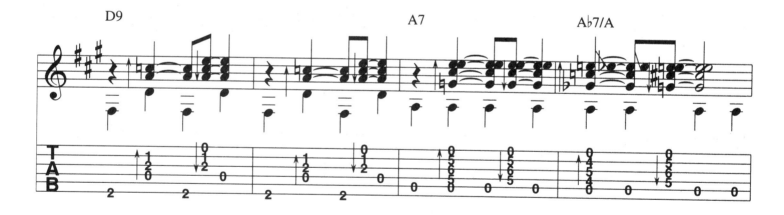

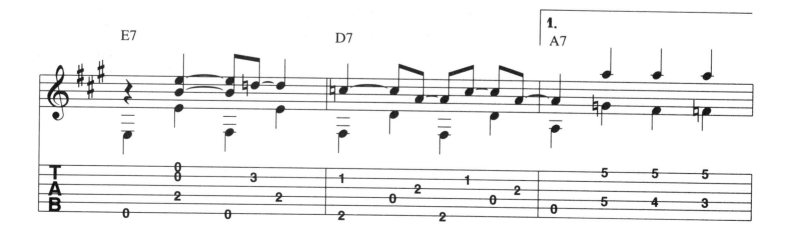

Additional lyrics

2. I said, Oh baby, where's you spend the night?

   I said, Oh baby, where's you spend the night?

   You come in this mornin' and you ain't lookin' right.

3. I'm gonna shoot my pistol, gonna shoot my girl and gone.

   I'm gonna shoot my pistol, gonna shoot my girl and gone.

   You made me love you, now look what you have done.

4. Got a .38 special, boys, and it do very well.

   Got a .38 special, boys, and it do very well.

   I've got a 32-20, and it's a-burning.

5. If she gets unruly, thinks she don't want me.

   If she gets unruly, thinks she don't want me.

   Take my 32-20 and cut her half in two.

6. She's got a .38 special but I believe it's most too light.

   She's got a .38 special but I believe it's most too light.

   I've got a 32-20, got to make the cats alright.

BLACK RAT SWING

This is a piece that Mark learned from John Cephas while Mark was playing at the Augusta Bluesweek. It is an excellent example of what is known as the "Piedmont" style of guitar picking. The Piedmont style came out of the mid-Atlantic states (the Carolinas, Maryland, etc.) and is brighter and more delicate than the Delta style. In many Piedmont blues tunes the performer will double her vocal melody on the guitar. You will notice also that this blues does not follow the usual format, but rather each verse takes up twenty-five bars. It was recorded in the 1940s by Memphis Minnie.

Musical Analysis

Other than its odd length, "Black Rat Swing" is fairly straightforward and should be easy enough if you have studied the section on melody notes. Notice the slides in measures 13 and 14, 22 and 23. Mark uses his middle finger to slide up to the fourth fret, then slides down to the second fret and uses his index finger on fret one, which puts him in position to play the E chord.

BLACK RAT SWING

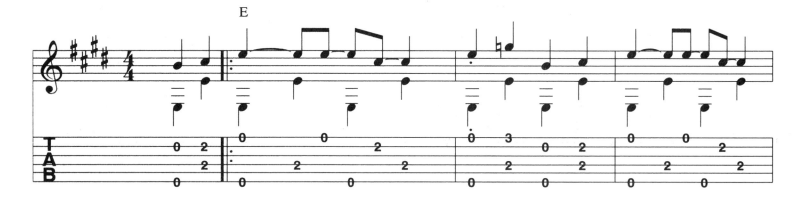

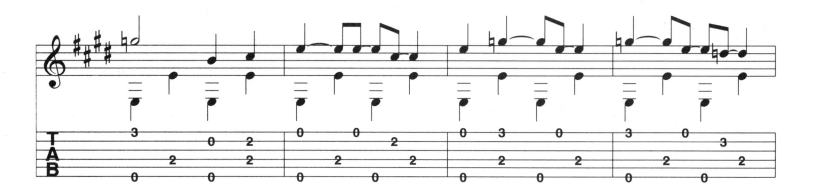

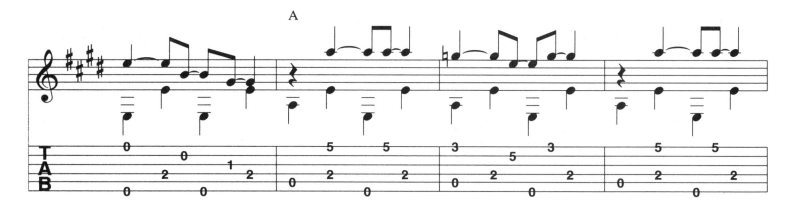

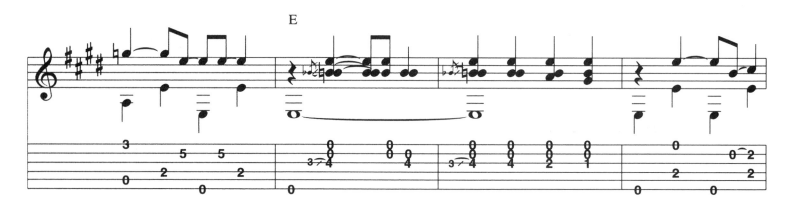

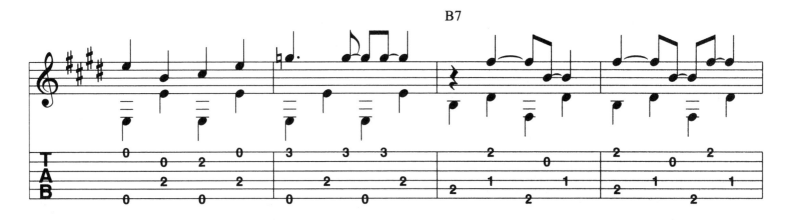

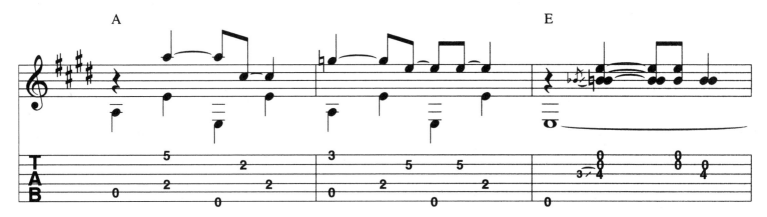

Additional lyrics

2. When you told me you loved me

    You done told me a lie,

    But still I love you girl until the day I die.

    You're just one black rat

    Someday I'm gonna catch your trail,

    Gonna hide my shoes

    Somewhere beneath your shirt-tail.

CONTENTS OF COMPACT DISC

On this recording, Mark plays through just about all of the exercises and pieces printed in the book, and he gives some extra explanation of some of the concepts and techniques you have read about. Below is a guide to the sequence of segments on the CD, along with the page numbers of their corresponding sections in the book.